The Young Country Doctor Book 16
Bilbury Mixture

Vernon Coleman

Another collection of memories relating to the village of Bilbury, and its inhabitants.

Note: Names and details of individuals and establishments have been altered to protect the innocent, the guilty and, in Peter Marshall's case, the not quite sure but whichever it is there will be a 5% discount on alternate Thursdays when there is a 'Q' in the month.

To Antoinette

You are the only past I remember, the only present that matters and the only future I want.

Foreword

I decided, a few months ago, to write a new book about Bilbury – simply because I still love the village and the villagers and I find it immensely enjoyable and relaxing to write about my experiences with friends such as Thumper Robinson and Patchy Fogg.

The Bilbury books are, of course, merely a peep into a continuum; a glimpse into a world that lives brightly in real life as well as in the mind and the memory.

In real life, the villagers are there all the time, doing whatever they are doing when I'm not writing about them and no one is reading about them.

And although I have changed the name to protect the village's privacy, Bilbury still exists, unchanged.

It is the village where Antoinette and I still live.

Here is yet more proof that life is stranger than fiction. I doubt if anyone could make up some of the stories in this book and I certainly wish that I were a good enough writer to do so.

The fact is that there are far more secrets around us than most people think. As a GP in a small, confined community I was privy to far more secrets than most people.

Country general practice is a drama that never ends.

I hope you enjoy reading this instalment of Bilbury history as much as I enjoyed remembering it. The stories are set at slightly different times and in varying seasons.

Vernon Coleman
Bilbury

Tickety Tonk

A cassette tape was playing on a small portable machine and the operating theatre was full of the sound of *My Fair Lady*.

Mr Berkeley Frampton, the surgeon, was clearly a fan of musicals.

I have always found surgeons to be rather unusual people.

For a start, the men and women who train to become surgeons work for six or seven years to acquire the right to call themselves 'Doctor' but then spend another few years training to be surgeons so that they can lose the title 'Doctor' and revert to calling themselves 'Mister', 'Miss', 'Mrs' or 'Ms'.

This curious habit dates back more than a century to the days when medically qualified men were all members of the Royal College of Physicians. These eminent physicians confined themselves to taking pulses, using leeches and prescribing drugs.

On the other hand, the men (and in those days they were all men) who wielded sharp knives and performed operations were barber surgeons who had no real medical qualifications. A barber surgeon would have found himself in the stocks (or worse) if he'd dared to call himself 'doctor'.

So Berkeley Frampton was Mr Frampton (unless he wanted to book a restaurant table, in which case he would swallow his pride and become Dr Frampton again).

A young student nurse, who had probably dreamt of higher things, had been put in charge of changing the tapes and we'd just finished listening to Julie Andrews working her way through the surgeon's cassette copy of *The Sound of Music*. We were now listening to Miss Andrews and the Ensemble singing 'Wouldn't it be loverly'.

Which, indeed, it would have been if I had not been listening to it in an operating theatre.

The operation hadn't yet started but I was already dripping with sweat.

Some doctors find the operating theatre a peaceful, congenial place to work but I never have. Even when I was a medical student I had known that I did not want to spend my professional life dressed in a mask and gown.

(A pal of mine always claimed that surgeons didn't really wear masks to prevent the spread of infection but so that the patient wouldn't know who had operated on them and wouldn't be able to sue them afterwards.)

To be perfectly honest, I do not find hospitals to be congenial places.

I worked in hospitals for several years but never really felt comfortable in them.

It's the smell, I think: that strange mixture of antiseptic, air freshener, polish, talcum powder, fear, sorrow and anaesthetic gases.

And the fact that, although the damned places always look clean enough, I know (because a pathologist told me) that the average hospital ward contains more deadly bugs per square inch than the average toilet bowl.

My day had not started well.

In the mail, before I left Bilbury Grange, I had received a set of laboratory results from the hospital. One of the reports gave me the startling and awful news that a patient of mine, Hamilton Murray, had lung cancer.

I had sent Hamilton to the hospital for an X-ray because he had a persistent cough and a pain in his chest. My first thought was that the cough was partly a result of a bout of flu and partly a result of the fact that he smoked at least 40 unfiltered cigarettes a day. I wanted an X-ray just to make sure that there was nothing more sinister going on. He'd been unwilling to go to the hospital and it had taken me nearly a month to persuade him to have the X-ray. In the end, he'd only agreed to go as a favour to me.

But the X-ray report made it clear that my worst fears were justified. Hamilton Murray had lung cancer.

On the way to the hospital, I called in to his home to tell him the news, and to promise that I would arrange an appointment for him to see a consultant to discuss all the therapeutic possibilities.

Hamilton has never married and lives alone in a tiny, one bedroom cottage which, for absolutely no good reason and with a false grandiosity based entirely upon a delightful sense of humour, he has renamed Barrington Court.

Visitors who are expecting to find a large, listed Elizabethan manor house, surrounded by a moat and mentioned in the appropriate volume of *Pevsner's*, are invariably startled to find that the tiny hovel they assume to be a lodge house is, in fact, Barrington Court.

Hamilton has a beard which bears a resemblance to a moth-eaten merkin and his clothes fit him a mite too soon. His wardrobe does not contain much in the way of elasticated beige and he tends to dress in colours which are what Jeeves, Bertie Wooster's butler, would have described as 'sudden'. He does this quite deliberately. He spends a lot of his time in woodlands and after an unfortunate accident when he was shot by a myopic marksman who thought he'd spotted a deer, he made a deliberate decision to wear brightly coloured clothes.

He gets his water from a well in his garden and his 'facilities' consist of a cesspit which is situated rather too close to the well for my liking. The cesspit is housed within a ramshackle wooden shed. The acre of land which surrounds the cottage has been completely stripped of anything that could possibly be used or sold as winter fuel. The bees whose hives decorate Hamilton's land have to travel into neighbouring woodland to collect nectar. It was Hamilton who taught me that it is important not to take all the honey from a hive. Bees need some of their honey to preserve and protect their own immune systems, and they will die if all their honey is taken.

Born in Edinburgh, but of English parentage, he went to Eton and trained as an architect, intending to follow in his father's footsteps.

His public school background, and an intense affection for the stories of P.G.Wodehouse has given him a delightfully old-fashioned vocabulary. His conversations are spattered with phrases such as 'Odds bodkins', 'Toodle pip', Tally ho' and 'Tickety tonk'.

Most remarkably, he has an extraordinary talent which enables him to imitate bird sounds with great skill. Every February he does cuckoo impersonations and on two separate occasions, visitors to North Devon have had letters published in *The Times* newspaper claiming that they've heard the first cuckoo of spring, when in truth they'd heard Hamilton having a little harmless fun with them.

After three months working in his father's practice, Hamilton decided that he hated the profession for which he had trained so assiduously and, after receiving a very small legacy from a distant relative, he travelled south in search of an escape from modern living and those aspects of civilisation which he regarded as oppressive and uncivilised.

When he quit his job he was low, miserable, almost depressed by a life which seemed to him to be too full of disappointments and frustrations.

He and his family did not see eye to eye and, from what I had learned, I suspect that the separation was as welcome to the one side as to the other.

I am always fascinated by the way individuals make vital, life-forming decisions on a whim. On simple, relatively unimportant issues we take advice, we read, we study, we consider before making our choices. We spend hours looking at the various options before buying a washing machine or a motor car. But the important things are often decided without any great thought at all. We all reach many crossroads in our lives and often choose the road we will take without any real thought about where it might take us.

Hamilton once admitted to me that he had ended up in Bilbury as a result of a series of chance encounters.

When leaving Edinburgh, he had taken a train to Leeds because he had thought he'd seen a girl he knew buy a ticket for that train. In fact he had been mistaken; the girl merely looked slightly like someone he knew.

After two days in Leeds, he had headed south because it hadn't stopped raining and the small hotel where he'd been staying was cold, dark and dismal.

He'd taken the first train south, and the train had led him to Birmingham.

He had stayed in Birmingham for a week and then, after seeing a poster advertising holidays in Devon, had decide that if he was going to be miserable he might just as well be miserable somewhere beautiful.

So he had taken a bus to Exeter.

From Exeter he'd taken the small train north to Barnstaple for no better reason than he wanted to spend another hour or so in the company of a woman he'd met in the railway buffet.

The additional hour had demolished any prospect of romance and after a week in Barnstaple, Hamilton had headed east, meaning to visit the twin towns of Lynton and Lynmouth.

But he never reached Lynton or Lynmouth.

He'd got off the bus when he had seen a signpost for Bilbury, confusing the name with Bibury, a famously picturesque village just north of Cirencester in Gloucestershire. Bibury stands on the river Coln, a tributary of the Thames, and Hamilton had seen many photographs of the famous Cotswold stone cottages on Arlington Row.

And it was in Bilbury that his journey had ended.

Hamilton had fallen in love, not with a girl or a woman, but with a village and a lifestyle.

He had, he once told me, decided that he would stay in Bilbury because he had had his best night's sleep for weeks at the Duck and Puddle. It wasn't the bed, he said, but the feeling of peace he felt. He told me that there is an old Irish saying that the beginning of a ship is a board, the beginning of a kiln is a stone and the beginning of health is sleep.

I like Hamilton very much.

He had a gently mischievous sense of humour.

A few years ago, he spent a summer working at a holiday camp in Ilfracombe and when one large family of holidaymakers turned out to be unpleasant, aggressive and consistently rude, both to the staff and to other holidaymakers, he dealt with them by throwing cold chips onto the roof of their caravan late at night.

He obtained the cold chips from the rubbish bins outside the mobile fish and chip van which parked in the campsite every evening.

Throwing bits of food onto a caravan roof is a favourite trick among those who work on caravan sites. It is the one good reason for never annoying the locals when you're spending your nights in a vehicle with a thin metal roof.

The bemused holidaymakers realised that the noise that woke them at 6 a.m. every morning was the sound of seagulls walking, pecking and squabbling on the thin metal roof of their holiday home,

9

but they never realised that the seagulls were on their roof because of the chips. And they certainly never knew that Hamilton had been the cause of their early morning wake up calls.

I'd been lucky to catch Hamilton at home.

Actually, 'lucky' wasn't the right word. As things turned out, it certainly wasn't lucky at all.

Like many people in Bilbury, Hamilton doesn't have one job (in the way that people in towns and cities usually have one job) but earns his living in a variety of different ways.

In the autumn and the winter, he wanders around the countryside on a bicycle with a small trailer attached to it. He doesn't own a vehicle which has a motor, though he drove a tank during the Second World War and his driving licence, which he once showed me, entitles him to drive one still, if he can ever find one available.

Whenever he sees a fallen tree or branch, Hamilton stops his bicycle, takes an old bow saw out of his trailer and cuts up the tree or branch into logs suitably sized to fit an ordinary hearth or log burner. I've known him take a week to cut up and cart away a small tree.

He has a number of regular customers to whom he delivers logs and kindling. The fallen trees and branches are sometimes on bits of wasteland and sometimes on land that belongs to someone who isn't bothering to do anything with it. No one ever objects to Hamilton chopping up the dead wood; on the contrary he is regarded as a useful scavenger, cleaning up and tidying the countryside and providing the villagers with an essential supply of fuel.

He once told me that willow trees (famous as the original source of aspirin and as the raw material from which cricket bats can be made) are his favourite source of kindling for they constantly shed small branches which can easily be snapped by hand into stove and hearth sized lengths.

In the summer, Hamilton sells newspapers, magazines and snacks to holidaymakers on the beach at Combe Martin.

He fills his trailer with suitable reading matter, nibbles and drinks at Peter Marshall's shop and rides his bicycle down to the beach. There he sells what he can before riding back to Peter's shop and unloading the unsold impedimenta. Peter pays Hamilton a small commission, a very modest percentage of the takings, for his labours.

I doubt if any of Hamilton's customers guess that the oddly dressed cyclist from whom they have bought their paperback, crisps and fizzy drink has a first class from Oxford University and is an Eton educated, qualified architect.

As a result of this healthy outdoor lifestyle, I have always thought Hamilton to be one of the fittest men I know. In a village where many of the residents lead healthy outdoor lives that is some distinction.

Sadly, however, Hamilton smokes.

In order to keep down his expenditure, he rolls his own cigarettes and smokes far too many of them a day. I sometimes think that by putting high taxes on all cigarettes, including the filtered ones, the Government is actually doing more harm than good.

Quite a few of my patients who smoke, buy their tobacco in tins and make their own cigarettes. Naturally, this means that the cigarettes they smoke are often far worse for their health than the cigarettes manufactured in bulk.

'I'll do everything I can,' I promised him when I'd told him the bad news about the X-ray.

'How long have I got?' he asked. 'Tell me the truth, doctor!'

Do people really want to know when they say this?

It is a question I have fought to answer since I became a doctor. Many patients say they want the truth but they don't. They cannot and do not deal with the truth. Would any of us really like to know when we will die? Should the doctor lie a little, perhaps? Should the doctor, at the very least, leave some hope – even though he may know, in his heart, that there is none?

Or is it true, as some would say, that there is always hope? After all, miracles do happen.

When I worked in hospital, I once had a patient who insisted that he be told the truth about his condition. The consultant, after a moment's hesitation, told him. It was not good news. The man became gloomy, depressed and obsessed with death. He made no plans for his family. He did nothing to tidy up his affairs. He merely sank into a state of paralysis. And he stayed that way until he died three months later. Would he have been better off not knowing? Should the consultant have sanitised the truth, lightened the prognosis a little, given some hope?

The one thing for sure is that there are no simple answers.

Every time the question is asked the doctor must, I believe, make a fresh decision; analyse all the evidence and everything he knows about the patient, his circumstances, his state of mind, his family and friends and so on. It is for this reason that I believe that an old-fashioned GP is the best person to answer the question, and to decide whether or not the truth should be told and if so how much of it should be shared.

I remember a patient of mine, a woman, who was dying of cancer.

From the start her husband, who had guessed the truth, begged me not to tell her. He said that she would not be able to cope with the truth. He insisted that he would shoulder the burden. And so I had kept the truth from her. I had accepted his advice.

But towards the end of her life, she had held my hand and she had smiled and she had told me that she had known all along, right from the moment when the diagnosis had been made, that she was dying.

'I appreciate you not telling us,' she said. 'My husband would never have been able to cope with the truth.'

She was convinced that I had kept the truth from her to protect her husband!

After that conversation I decided that I had, perhaps, made a mistake. I should have told her and then we could have talked more. Maybe I could have offered her more help.

And after she died, I knew that I had made an error. I had been wrong.

The minute she died, before the funeral took place, her husband began to wallow in a sense of martyrdom. He had, he told everyone who would listen, shouldered the burden of his wife's diagnosis by himself because she would not have been strong enough to deal with the truth. He was submerged in waves of sympathy; for being a widower and for having borne the burden by himself; for having protected his 'weak' wife from reality.

But the truth was that they had both known.

And she had suffered alone and in silence to protect her husband.

After his wife's death he enjoyed the sympathy of their relatives, friends and neighbours for three months and then, suddenly, he announced that he was marrying his ex-wife's best friend.

I told Hamilton Murray the truth about his illness. I told him everything I knew.

I've known him for years and he has always seemed to me to be a man who likes straight talk. He is not the sort of man to tiptoe round a difficult topic or to be put off by the prospect of embarrassing a friend or a neighbour.

I told him that according to the X-ray report, the prognosis was not good but nor was it dire. 'I'll get you an appointment with a surgeon,' I told him. 'If, as the X-ray suggests, the lump in your lung hasn't spread, then it may be possible for a surgeon to operate and remove it. It's a large lump but it might be possible to remove it.'

I tried to be as upbeat as it is possible to be when telling a man who smokes that he has cancer of the lung. I promised I would do everything possible to help him.

He was not impressed by the prospect of an operation. He told me point blank that he would rather die than have an operation.

'I hate hospitals,' he said, with a shudder, taking out his tobacco pouch and starting to roll a fresh cigarette. I remembered how difficult it had been to persuade him to go to the hospital to have an X-ray.

And I kept thinking of Hamilton as I stood waiting for the operation to begin.

'She's all yours,' said Alston Churchill, the anaesthetist, who was sitting at the head of the operating table, no more than eighteen inches away from the patient's head. He seemed very young, in his late twenties, but he already had that quiet, calming confidence which is a hallmark of the professional anaesthetist. He was a keen walker and I'd seen him in the Duck and Puddle a couple of times.

'Right!' said the surgeon. He looked around. 'Do you know who this is?'

Puzzled, the anaesthetist looked up at him.

'Singing,' explained the surgeon. 'Who's singing?'

The anaesthetist thought for a moment. 'Audrey Hepburn?'

The surgeon laughed. 'You're a bloody Philistine, Churchill! This is the sound track of the stage version and Julie Andrews is playing Eliza Doolittle.' The surgeon paused and wagged a gloved finger at the anaesthetist. 'Interesting mistake though,' he said. 'Miss Hepburn took the part in the film version but apart from the first verse of 'Just You Wait, Henry Higgins' her singing was dubbed by a woman called Marni Nixon who was a very interesting and talented singer who did the singing for Deborah Kerr in *The King*

13

and I, for Sophia Loren in *Boy on a Dolphin* and for Natalie Wood in *West Side Story.* She also did the high notes for Marilyn Monroe in *Diamonds are a Girl's Best Friend.*'

All this information was greeted with murmurings as we all showed how impressed we were. The last thing anyone in an operating theatre wants to do is to upset the surgeon.

'Funnily enough,' said the surgeon, now thoroughly warmed up in his temporary role as an expert on musicals, 'Marni Nixon actually appears on screen in *The Sound of Music.* She plays one of the nuns.'

'Golly', said the anaesthetist, trying to sound interested.

'Are you all set?' asked the surgeon, reverting to his day job. 'Everyone comfortable?'

No one spoke.

'Are we all ready to go?' asked the surgeon, slightly irritated by the lack of response to his previous question.

To be honest I couldn't tell when his questions required an answer or were simply rhetorical. He had that odd habit of allowing his voice to rise at the end of every sentence, turning everything he said into a question. So when there was a question which required an answer I didn't reply straight away. He probably just thought I was a little slow-witted. I was, however, slightly reassured by the fact that no one else had replied to him.

The theatre sister standing beside me then muttered something which I took to be an assent.

She had been built by the same firm which built the concrete block houses which were erected during the Second World War, and which still decorate the English coastline. She had a bust which looked large enough and firm enough to support a couple of anti-aircraft guns.

She didn't seem quite as full of jollity as the surgeon. In fact, she looked as if she'd eaten something which had disagreed with her and was now winning the argument.

Another nurse stood at the head of the operating table, with a tray full of surgical implements at her side. The instruments, neatly laid out and all fresh from the autoclave, were shiny and all carefully positioned so that the nurse could pick out whatever the surgeon requested.

A third nurse, who was not scrubbed, was standing a yard or two away ready to turn lights on or off, fiddle with the air conditioning system or fetch bits and pieces which might turn out to be necessary. It was also her job to collect discarded equipment and swabs and to keep a count of them as they were used.

The nurse who was in charge of operating the cassette player was clearly very junior and was, I assumed, simply there to observe, to learn and to try not to faint.

The patient, Miss Barley, was lying on her tummy and most of her back was covered with sterile green towels. The only part of her that was visible was her bottom which looked very pink and which was indubitably of the economy sized family pack variety.

I had only been in the operating theatre for a few minutes but I had already developed an itch at the back of my neck and, because the white rubber surgical boots I had borrowed were two sizes too small, my feet were complaining bitterly about their incarceration.

I was in the operating theatre because Miss Barley, one my patients, needed surgery, and had refused to go to the hospital unless I promised to be present during the operation.

'I trust you doctor,' said Miss Barley. 'I'd feel safe if I knew you were performing the operation.'

I had explained that I could not possibly perform the operation she required.

'I'm a GP,' I told her. 'The surgeon to whom I referred you is very competent. He will be the one who'll do the operation.'

'But if you're there, you'll be able to keep an eye on things won't you? You're a doctor, you'll be able to take over if you think he's doing something wrong.'

At that time it was the case that once a doctor was qualified he could, without any additional training or qualifications, take on any post or responsibilities for which he felt himself adequately prepared. There was nothing in law to stop me performing the operation myself.

I had explained to Miss Barley that although there was no legal reason why I couldn't perform her operation it would be quite inappropriate of me to do anything other than be there to hold her hand when she was anaesthetised, and to be there when she came round after the operation was over.

My original plan had been to fulfil my promise by putting on theatre scrubs and a surgical cap and mask and standing quietly in a corner but when I had asked the surgeon if he minded if I joined him in the theatre, he had insisted that I go the whole hog; scrub up, put on the rubber gloves and join him at the table as his assistant.

'My house surgeon is down with some nasty bug,' he had told me. 'If you scrub up then my registrar can cover the out-patients list.'

I had protested that it had been some time since I'd been in an operating theatre, let alone done any holding, pulling and snipping (the three basic tasks of the assistant surgeon are holding bits of the patient that are in danger of getting in the way, pulling organs and tissues which are interfering with the field of play and snipping bits of tissue or sutures as and when required) but the surgeon had dismissed my reticence as irrelevant.

'You can't do worse than my bloody house surgeon. He's a handsome looking devil but between the aquiline nose and the receding chin at the front and the cascade of golden curls at the back there is a complete vacuum. Heaven knows how he got through medical school. I only took him on as a favour to his father. I can't even trust him with a pair of scissors, let alone a scalpel.'

'They say Napoleon liked to surround himself with lucky men,' continued the surgeon. 'I seem to get lumbered with unlucky bastards as house surgeons. The last three I've had have all been clumsy, stupid and unlucky. If they'd won the pools they'd have lost the coupon. Just keep your elbows out of my way and remember to laugh at my jokes,' he said merrily. 'I like a bit of banter in the operating theatre. It helps to keep me awake.'

This was not, I confess, the best of news.

Some surgeons like to concentrate on the work in hand. They approach their work with all the earnest caution of bomb disposal experts.

But others regard the second word of the phrase 'operating theatre' as an invitation to display their talent as stand-up comedians with the certain and doubtless comforting knowledge that there is one huge difference between the professional stand-up comedian.

The professional comedian is a fellow who must take his life in his mouth every time he steps out on stage. He is constantly desperate for the first laugh.

The surgeon, on the other hand, knows damned well that he is in charge and can expect his audience to laugh and titter at all the appropriate moments.

The junior doctor who is hoping for a good reference when he applies for his next job will know that it is his job to lead the rest in providing suitably appreciative noises when the consultant cracks what he think is a joke, or allows a witty remark to escape.

'What do you think, shall we give her a nice tattoo?' asked the surgeon. 'Something tasteful, of course. A little extra? A memento for our lucky patient.'

The theatre sister ignored him. The junior nurses giggled. I couldn't believe what I'd heard. Was he serious?

'What's our patient's name?' the surgeon asked the theatre sister.

'Miss Marigold Barley,' replied the theatre sister, rather coldly. 'She's 57-years-old and has no listed allergies.'

The sister didn't know but Miss Barley is, not unnaturally, known in the village as 'Pearl'. I don't think I've ever heard anyone call her Marigold.

Miss Andrews had now been replaced by Stanley Holloway, who was playing Alfred P. Doolittle, and he and an impromptu choir of his fellow dustmen were all heartily singing 'With a Little Bit of Luck'.

The surgeon looked over his mask at me. 'Is Miss Barley married? Engaged? Suitor? String of ardent boyfriends?'

'None of those,' I replied. 'She's a rather prim and very proper maiden lady who does a lot of good works in the village and for the local church.'

'So the only organ she's familiar with is the one in the church, eh?'

'Probably,' I agreed.

'Then no one will ever know if we give her a tattoo, will they?' said the surgeon. 'And unless she's in the habit of examining her very fine rear in a mirror she'll certainly never know. What do you think, doctor? You're her GP. You know her well. Should we decorate her with a nice tattoo of a sailing ship, disappearing over the horizon of the left buttock? Or a fox, perhaps, going to earth? Or do you think a nice, single red rose would be more appropriate?'

He paused, as though in thought.

'No, the fox would be best; a handsome Mr Reynard disappearing to safety, with a large bushy tail waving behind him.'

I looked at the surgeon.

I still wasn't entirely sure just how serious he was being.

The suggestion was, to say the least, outrageous, unprofessional and illegal and I was not prepared to allow him to tattoo one of my patients. Even though they might never see the tattoo, I would know it was there and that I had been there when the evil deed had been done.

Could he really be serious?

Although Mr Frampton had a reputation as an excellent and skilful surgeon, he also had a reputation for being a trifle unconventional in his approach to life but I did not know him well enough to know whether or not he was joking.

Although still only in his thirties, he had been married three times and after being caught by the local police for driving while under the influence of alcohol he had managed to keep hold of his driving licence only by hiring an expensive, skilled QC.

The barrister had flattered the local magistrates by his very presence and had argued that if the surgeon lost his licence, he would be unable to attend to his patients in emergency situations.

'The inevitable delay engendered by waiting for a public taxi to arrive could well prove fatal to some unfortunate patient,' the QC had argued. 'My clients skilful hands are required on demand, not five or ten minutes hence.'

The magistrates, putty in the barrister's very capable hands, had charged the surgeon £10 and politely asked him not to do it again.

'Where's the tattoo kit, sister?' asked the surgeon. 'My needles and coloured inks!'

'I don't know,' replied the sister, rather huffily. 'Maybe they're in your rooms at the private hospital.'

She was clearly neither amused nor impressed by Mr Frampton's irreverent banter.

The surgeon, like most of his colleagues, kept a suite of rooms at a local private hospital where he performed the same sort of operations as he performed at the NHS hospital. The only real difference was that at the private hospital the surgeon was allowed to charge very sizeable fees.

The surgeon sighed. 'Ah well, another good idea bites the dust. Better get on with what we're here for. What does Miss Barley want from us today? A Caesarian section to deliver a surprise bouncing boy? A breast enhancement operation to boost her chances at the church social? Twenty minutes of liposuction to turn her thighs sylphlike and girlish?'

'She's got internal haemorrhoids,' said the theatre sister, in a very matter of fact voice. 'I think she would like you to get rid of them for her.'

She had been busily painting Miss Barley's buttocks with an antiseptic solution which had temporarily stained them reddish brown. She had painted with great care and delicacy, gently moving the draped green towels so that every square inch of exposed skin was sterilised.

'Ah, piles!' cried the surgeon merrily. 'Let's take a look at the field of play!'

He reached down, parted the cheeks of Miss Barley's buttocks and peered at the spot the tattooed fox would have been aiming for had the surgeon continued with his plan.

'How's your yacht, Alston?' he suddenly demanded.

'It's not exactly a yacht,' said the anaesthetist.

'He's got a bloody yacht, you know!' said the surgeon, addressing me. 'They earn a fortune these bloody gas men. Wish I could afford a yacht.'

The surgeon stuck a gloved finger into Miss Barley's anal sphincter and moved it around, stretching the sphincter muscle before adding a second finger.

It had been a while since I'd been in an operating theatre, it all seemed to be a strange mixture of the impersonal and the humiliating. Some surgeons do tend to see their patients as little more than collections of tissue and organs. Poor Miss Barley; she would have died of shame if she hadn't been unconscious.

'It's 17 foot long for heaven's sake,' said the anaesthetist. 'It's really no more than a rather grand dinghy. It's got a tiny cabin and an outboard motor. If I lie down in the cabin my feet stick out through the door.'

'I think he uses it for smuggling,' said the surgeon, speaking to me and ignoring the anaesthetist. 'I'll bet he sails in at the dead of night in order to avoid the customs people. He doubtless has the thing packed to the gunwales with Italian wine, Belgian chocolates and French cigarettes. I bet he makes another fortune out of it all.'

He bent closer to Miss Barley's bottom and poked at it with a gloved finger. 'There are just two rather nasty little chaps here. I think we'll get rid of them both with the rubber band machine. Have you seen the rubber band machine in action? Did they have them when you were a student? Give me the anal speculum and the rubber band machine please, sister.'

The surgeon had segued so fast from talking about the anaesthetist's boat to discussing Miss Barley's piles and requesting the equipment to deal with them that I was in danger of losing the plot.

'Yes, oh yes, they had the rubber band ligator,' I said.

I remembered one of the consultant surgeons at the teaching hospital where I trained showing us the ligator.

It was a brand new invention at the time and he was unnaturally proud of it.

It consisted of a specially designed pair of forceps which enabled the surgeon to fire a rubber band around the base of the haemorrhoid. Once in position the rubber band cut off the blood supply to the haemorrhoid, causing it to shrivel up and drop off in a day or two. Prior to the invention of the rubber band ligation technique, the annihilation of haemorrhoids was a rather crude business which, to put it bluntly, simply involved hacking them out with a sharp knife and then sewing up what was left over.

'We could have done this in out-patients,' said the surgeon. 'Didn't need a full anaesthetic and all this folderol.'

'Miss Barley is very nervous,' I reminded him. 'And she lives alone. She really wouldn't have been a suitable patient for out-patient surgery. And you did say to her that if she came into the hospital you'd be able to deal with everything in one go.'

'Hmm,' said the surgeon, taking the anal speculum, (a piece of equipment which is also known as an anoscope and which is, in reality, little more than a very expensive short metal tube) and the rubber band machine off the theatre sister.

He put them both down on the sterile green cloths covering the patient's lower back.

'It's crowded with two people in the cabin,' said the anaesthetist, wearily and defensively. 'My wife and I never take it out of the Taw estuary. We use it for bird watching.'

He didn't seem to realise that the surgeon had been teasing him.

'Birds, eh?' said the surgeon, with a guffaw. 'I wager it's bloody cold on that estuary of yours. I bet all you see are blue tits, eh, what do you think sister?'

'I wouldn't know Mr Frampton,' said the sister, rather coldly.

She was clearly accustomed to the surgeon's manner and was not going to allow herself to be drawn into his rather bizarre world of imagination, double entendre and insult.

'My wife paints them and I take photographs,' explained the anaesthetist wearily.

'You play golf?' the surgeon demanded, suddenly switching targets and subjects. He was still dealing with Miss Barley's piles.

It took me a moment to realise that he was talking to me.

'I tried once,' I said.

'I thought all GPs played golf. Couple of chaps I know play all the time. They have trainees or assistants or whatever you call them and leave them to do all the work while they bugger off and play golf.'

'I don't have an assistant,' I pointed out. 'And I don't have any partners.'

'So no golf, eh?'

'A chap I know lent me some clubs and I played a round when I was at medical school,' I told him. 'But I think they'd put all the greens in the wrong places. I found them far too small. Added to which the balls they sold me were fitted with some sort of homing device which took them straight into the long grass every time I hit them. I decided golf wasn't for me. I seem to remember the chap I was playing with and I both ran out of balls and we just walked back to the clubhouse after the 12th hole.'

The surgeon made a snorting noise.

I could not tell whether he approved or disapproved of my failure as a golfer.

Mr Holloway and his chums finished celebrating as the surgeon picked up the anal speculum.

As Rex Harrison started to sing 'I'm an Ordinary Man' the surgeon held the speculum up so that the theatre sister could add a blob of grease, so that it would enter the target area more readily.

She did this without a word being exchanged.

I remembered noticing that a good theatre sister who has worked with a surgeon for a few years will know instinctively what he wants without anything being said.

In films about hospitals, the operating theatre banter is all of the 'Scalpel, nurse', 'Mop my brow nurse', 'Forceps, nurse' variety, but in real life the conversation is more likely to include phrases such as 'Did you see that bizarre television programme about pearl fishermen?' or 'Do you think England should play Peter Shilton in goal on Saturday?'.

The surgeon placed the speculum in position and the theatre sister, unbidden, ordered the nurse who had not scrubbed and who was not wearing rubber surgical gloves, to direct a theatre light in such a way that Mr Frampton could see what he was doing and what needed to be done. This wasn't brain surgery but any sort of surgery can be dangerous. There is no such thing as 'minor surgery'.

The surgeon, who had joined in with Mr Rex Harrison and clearly knew all the words to this particular song, then picked up the rubber band ligator and fired a rubber band around one of the internal haemorrhoids. When that was done he did the second haemorrhoid. The whole procedure was over in considerably less time than it takes a kettle to boil.

'There we are,' said the surgeon. 'All done and dusted.'

He pulled the anal speculum from Miss Barley and handed it to the sister who handed it to the nurse who was looking after the discarded instruments.

He looked at me. 'Are you sure she wouldn't like a tasteful tattoo?'

He traced an area on Miss Barley's left buttock cheek. 'There's room here for something quite wonderful: a bucolic country scene, complete with a few sheep, a wind shaped tree and a raggedy shepherd. Or I could manage a three masted sailing schooner disappearing off across calm seas and heading towards a distant horizon.'

'I don't think she'd be properly appreciative,' I told him, rather nervously.

'Neither of those?'

'Neither.'

'No dragons, skulls, roses or memorials to 'Mother'?'

'No, I really don't think so.'

'Ah well,' sighed the surgeon.

I didn't think he was being serious but it was difficult to tell.

Mr Harrison finished talking his way through his song and after a momentary pause, Miss Andrews reappeared with a spirited rendition of 'Just You Wait'.

'You were wonderful,' said the surgeon, looking at me. 'I couldn't have managed without you.'

The theatre sister pulled the towels from the patient and handed them one by one to the nurse who was keeping score of all the bits and pieces of equipment which had been used during the operation. For a theatre sister there is nothing worse than getting to the end of an operation and discovering that a clamp or a sterile towel is missing. I've known a surgical team to spend the best part of an hour scouring an operating theatre for a missing swab and, in the end, having to open up the patient to search for the missing item.

The anaesthetist started to bring the patient back into the land of the conscious.

I hadn't done a single thing.

I hadn't held anything, pulled anything or snipped anything.

To be honest I felt a bit disappointed. I felt like a substitute who sits on the bench throughout a match and then doesn't quite know how much he should celebrate when his side is victorious.

'What's up next, sister?' asked the surgeon, pulling off his gloves.

'You've got Mr Wilkins, who needs his appendix removing and then you have Mrs Fanshaw for a cholecystectomy,' replied the theatre sister who appeared to have memorised the entire surgical list.

The surgeon turned to me. 'You know how to do an appendectomy, don't you?'

'I suppose so,' I said, hesitantly. 'I did a couple when I was a house surgeon.'

'Splendid,' said the surgeon, 'in that case you can do the appendix for me.' He tossed his gloves towards a waste bin, missing by several feet, and turned away. 'And I'll go and have a nice cup of tea and a bun. I didn't have time for breakfast and I'm starving.'

I stared after him, hoping that this, like the tattoo, was another of his jokes.

'He was joking wasn't he?' I said to the anaesthetist, who was supervising the removal of the patient from the operating table onto a trolley.

My mind started to whirl as I tried to remember precisely what I had to do.

Removing an appendix is one of the easiest operations there is, but things can and do go wrong. The appendix is very small, no bigger than a little finger, and it can sometimes be difficult to find.

'No, I don't think so,' replied the anaesthetist. 'I think he's gone for something to eat. He said he was going for a bun and a cup of tea. He never jokes about food.'

Rex Harrison, Julie Andrews and the actor who played Henry Higgins's chum started singing 'The Rain in Spain'.

'You'd better go and get re-scrubbed,' said the theatre sister, who had picked the surgeon's gloves off the floor and dropped them into the waste bucket. She then removed her own gloves and added them before reaching behind her and unfastening the ties on her gown.

I pulled off my gloves, walked across to the bin and dropped them in. 'Does he ever actually tattoo anyone?' I asked her.

'Good heavens no,' said the theatre sister. 'It's just one of his little jokes. He always does the tattoo thing whenever there's anyone new in theatre.'

The nurse who hadn't scrubbed up wheeled away the trolley containing all the used instruments and green drapes and as soon as she had left the operating theatre, another nurse wheeled in a replacement trolley upon which a fresh set of instruments had been laid out. The instruments were all covered with a sterile cloth but I could see them lying there, waiting for me.

I could also see the next patient, the one with the unwanted appendix, lying on a trolley in the small ante room to the operating theatre. I could hear the anaesthetist asking him to count down from one hundred.

Julie Andrews was now singing 'I Could Have Danced All Night' to Professor Higgins's housekeeper who was sensibly urging her to go bed.

The patient managed to count down to 96 before his voice tailed off. In my experience no one ever gets down to 90.

I had been nervous before. I was now utterly terrified. I could suddenly remember all the things that can go wrong with any operation. I tried to remember what vital blood vessels are located in the lower right quadrant of the abdomen where the appendix usually resides.

A jolly porter arrived pushing a trolley upon which lay the anaesthetised young man with the faulty appendix.

The anaesthetist, the same one who had just left the theatre, followed the trolley. He was wheeling a drip stand.

'Here's your new patient!' said the anaesthetist, brightly announcing the patient's arrival in the same jolly, optimistic sort of way that a restaurant waiter might announce the arrival of a special dish: a soufflé or a Christmas pudding covered in flaming brandy. 'Hadn't you better get scrubbed?'

Julie Andrews, presumably exhausted by now, had finished dancing all night and the show company were well into the Ascot Gavotte.

I hurried out of the theatre to get scrubbed.

And there I found the surgeon waiting for me.

'You still here?' he said, looking surprised.

'I thought you wanted me to…,' I stuttered.

He laughed. The theatre sister, who was standing nearby did not exactly laugh. But she smiled.

'You don't?' I said.

'Have you looked at the date today?'

'It's April…' I said, and then the penny dropped.

'…the first,' said the surgeon.

The sense of relief was extraordinary.

I felt as though I had been standing on the steps to the gallows and had received a last minute pardon from the Home Secretary.

'Of course if you'd like to remove an appendix…' he said.

'No, no, no!' I said quickly. 'That's fine. Thank you for asking but I think my operating days are over.'

I felt too strong a sense of relief to feel any sort of a fool.

We all have our strengths and our weaknesses.

I could cope well enough if faced with a badly injured patient in a field, in the rain, in the dark and with help more than an hour away.

But put me in a sterile, neat hospital operating theatre and ask me to perform a simple, routine operation and I start to fall apart.

Strange isn't it?

My only comfort was the vague and possibly simply self-serving thought that maybe even the skilled hospital surgeon might occasionally find the life of a lone GP to be a challenge too far.

'Come and say hello to your patient,' said the surgeon.

I followed him out into a corridor.

All British hospitals have wide corridors.

When they were built, the idea was that the corridors had to be wide enough for two trolleys to pass without colliding. These days, there is such a shortage of space that corridors are used for storing patients. And the corridors approaching an operating theatre are invariably clogged with patients who have been parked. Some are waiting to go into the operating theatre and some have just left.

Miss Barley was awake lying on a trolley.

'How are you feeling?' I asked her.

'Woozy,' she replied, sounding woozy. 'When am I going to the theatre to have this problem dealt with?'

She still didn't have her teeth in, and that and the anaesthetic resulted in her sounding quite unlike her normal self.

'It's been done!' I told her.

'Your doctor did a terrific job,' said the surgeon.

'I didn't actually…' I tried to interrupt.

'Marvellous work,' said the surgeon. 'I just stood there and watched. But he didn't need me at all. I could have stayed at home and had a leisurely breakfast.'

Miss Barley looked delighted.

I felt embarrassed.

The surgeon winked and headed back to theatre to remove an appendix.

In the distance, I could hear the sound of Freddy Eynsford-Hill, who has followed Eliza home, lustily singing 'On the Street Where You Live'.

I said goodbye to Miss Barley, told her I would pop in to see her the following day and headed for the exit door on my way back home and back to being a general practitioner.

Just as I was about to climb into the Rolls Royce, a woman in a white coat came running out towards me waving a piece of paper. I didn't recognise her but she wore a white coat with one of those little blue badges that people wear when they work in the radiology department, so that their exposure to X-rays can be monitored. Since I knew the two radiologists at the hospital she was obviously one of the radiographers.

'We posted you an X-ray report about Mr Hamilton Murray,' she said, rather breathlessly.

'I got it this morning,' I said. 'It was very sad news.'

'You haven't said anything to the patient, have you?'

'I called in on my way here and told him,' I said. 'I want to get on with fixing up a treatment programme as soon as possible.'

'Oh no, that's awful,' she said. She looked as if she were about to burst into tears. 'I'm afraid there's been a mistake. A terrible mistake.'

She told me that the report I had received had been written by one of the radiologists at the end of a long, tiring day and that he had mistaken an old tuberculosis scar for a new, cancerous lesion.

'Dr Clutterbuck always asks Dr Lloyd to take a look at the X-rays on which he has reported – just to check that there haven't been any mistakes. The two doctors check each other's X-rays to minimise the risk of error.' Dr Clutterbuck and Dr Lloyd were the hospital's two consultant radiologists.

'Mr Murray hasn't got cancer?' I said, delighted but wishing I had waited before breaking the news to him.

She shook her head. 'Dr Clutterbuck and Dr Lloyd are quite sure about it,' she said. She handed me a revised X-ray report. I looked at it. They were both certain that the lesion seen on the X-ray was an old tuberculosis scar and of no consequence.

I thanked her, put the report into my pocket and started the car, determined to get back to Bilbury as quickly as I could to give Hamilton the good news.

And then I got out of the car and rushed back into the hospital and went to the first telephone I could find.

It seemed to me that this was not news that could or should wait a second. Not for the first time in my life I found myself wondering if the telephone people would ever succeed in inventing a mobile telephone which could be used anywhere.

First, I had to telephone Bilbury Grange and obtain the correct phone number for Johnny Douglas, who has the cottage nearest to Hamilton. (Hamilton Murray does not, of course, have a telephone of his own.)

I rang Johnny's number.

There was no reply.

I let the phone ring for over a minute.

But no one answered.

I put the phone down, checked the number Miss Johnson had given me and dialled again, hoping that I had perhaps misdialled.

Again there was no reply.

I felt cold inside.

I don't know why but I had an awful foreboding.

I remembered a patient of Dr Brownlow's who had been given a diagnosis of cancer. He had been a veterinary surgeon and he had gone home and killed himself with a humane killer. He'd put the awful device to his temple and shot himself. His wife had found him slumped on the desk in his study.

I rushed out of the hospital, climbed back into the Rolls and headed back to Bilbury as fast as I dared go.

Why, I asked myself every few seconds, had I stopped to tell Hamilton about the X-ray report on my way to the hospital that morning?

It could have waited.

I thought about it and thought I knew the answer.

If it had been me I would have wanted to know as soon as possible so that I would have time to plan for the future. There are always so many things to think about and to do at such a time. Again and again I remembered Hamilton making me promise to tell him the truth the minute I knew it.

'No prevaricating,' he said. 'No clever, fancy language that tiptoes around the truth.'

I found a little comfort only in something which my predecessor Dr Brownlow had once told me to ask myself.

'When something goes wrong,' he said, 'you must ask yourself this question: 'Do I believe that I did the right thing?' It doesn't matter what happened, or even what other people think. What matters is your own answer to that question.'

As usual, I found the words of the late and much missed Dr Brownlow to be comforting.

When it was built, half a century earlier, the Rolls Royce 20/25 I had inherited from Dr Brownlow had not been designed to be hurled around narrow country lanes. Age had not made it any more suited to fast driving along the curling lanes of Devon with their high banks and blind corners. It was unseasonably cold too and there was still some frost on the road on shaded corners.

But the Gods were with me, and I got back to Bilbury without colliding with any oncoming traffic or sliding into a ditch or hedge.

I drove straight to Hamilton's tiny cottage and slid to a halt on the wet and muddy grass patch outside it.

The cottage, which is very small, was quite empty.

Like most of the people who live in Bilbury, Hamilton never locked his front door (indeed, I suspect that if you'd asked him to find the key he would have been hard pressed to do so) and so I walked in through the front door unhindered. I don't think anyone in Bilbury locks their doors. As far as Patsy and I are concerned, this is just as well since our iron front door key is 14 inches long and our back door key is slightly longer. Both weigh enough to make excellent paper weights – which is what we do with them.

There was no sign of my patient or his bicycle, though his small and ancient trailer, the one which he usually tows behind his bicycle, was still standing by the front door, half full of kindling.

I went through the rooms slowly, for a second time.

I don't know why I had expected a second search to be more productive but there was still no sign of him.

I even found myself looking on the kitchen table and on the sideboard in the small living room. I didn't like to admit it to myself but I was looking to see if he had written a note.

Hamilton is a man who lives a simple and structured life. If he is not at home then he will either be out collecting wood, delivering wood, selling stuff on the beach at Combe Martin or doing his shopping at Peter Marshall's shop. That's it. He doesn't frequent the Duck and Puddle, he doesn't go to church, he doesn't go visiting and as far as I know he never leaves North Devon. And whether he is in or out he always has his trailer fixed on to the back of his bicycle. I had never before seen the two separated. The weather was too cold for him to be selling anything on the beach. He clearly wasn't out collecting or delivering wood.

I began to have a very bad feeling.

Why, oh why could he have not been out when I had called at his cottage before leaving for Barnstaple? If he had been out I wouldn't have been able to tell him the false bad news.

29

But I had seen him.

And I had told him that he was dying when he wasn't.

My mind was racing as I tried to think where he could have gone and what he could be planning to do.

Actually, I thought I knew what he was planning to do.

I had a powerful suspicion that he had decided to end his life.

When you work as a country GP you get to know your patients well. City doctors measure their patients in the thousands, and they often live miles away from their consulting rooms and their patients. I measure my patients in the hundreds and I live amongst them.

When I'd seen him that morning, and had told him what I thought was the result of his X-ray examination, I had told Hamilton that I would see him later that day so that we could discuss possible forms of treatment. I had been as upbeat as possible. I had implied that a diagnosis of cancer was not the death sentence it sounded. I had tried to be optimistic.

But the corollary of my knowing my patients well is that they know me well too.

Maybe I hadn't been as clever as I thought I had been. Maybe Hamilton had suspected that I had been covering up the truth. Maybe he suspected that he had only a few weeks, even days, to live. What if he feared that the end would be painful and difficult?

Again and again I cursed myself for calling at his cottage that morning. And I cursed my bad luck in finding him in. Strangely, it never occurred to me to curse the radiologist who had made the mistake. No one makes mistakes on purpose.

Eventually, after a minute or two of this nonsense, I managed to pull myself together. There was no point in wasting time berating myself.

The task was simple: I had to try to find him. I had to work out where he might have gone, hunt him down and stop him harming himself. The fact that he wasn't in his cottage, and that he had left behind his bicycle trailer, strongly suggested to me that he'd gone somewhere quiet and peaceful where he could end his life.

He would want to be away from people. He didn't much like people. He would want to be somewhere quite alone. And how would he do it? Slit his wrists? Hang himself from a tree? Throw himself off a cliff? There are a hundred ways for anyone to kill themselves. I didn't think he would take tablets because I hadn't prescribed any for him and I didn't think he would have been able to get a supply from anyone else.

But what if he'd bought some aspirin tablets from Peter Marshall's shop? Some city pharmacists limit the number of aspirin tablets their customers can buy but Peter has never taken much notice of such bureaucracy. If he knows someone, and thinks them sane and sensible, he has always sold them as many tablets as they have asked for. If you have bad arthritis in your knees or hips and you have to walk three miles to the shop you don't want to have to go there three or four times a day.

And there was another possibility.

Maybe Hamilton had just popped down to Peter's shop to buy a loaf of bread.

I jumped back into the car and drove through the village to Peter Marshall's shop. It took me no more than five or six minutes.

'Have you seen Hamilton Murray today?' I asked Peter. He was arranging parsnips on a tray.

Peter looked at me. 'Funny you should ask,' he said, 'he was in here this morning. About three hours ago.'

'What did he buy?' I demanded.

'I'm not sure I should tell you that,' said Peter, with mock indignation. 'It's a question of shopkeeper-customer confidentiality. Would you like me to tell everyone what you buy?'

'Peter!' I shouted. 'What did Hamilton buy? I need to know. It's important.'

'That's another funny thing,' said Peter, immediately abandoning his high moral position. 'He bought a bottle of whisky. I can't remember when he last bought whisky. He bought one of the blended whiskies. I've got a special offer on several blended whiskies and he bought the Haig. He just stuffed the bottle in his jacket pocket.'

I felt hollow. I knew immediately what Hamilton was planning.

The weather was cold and the forecast was for a freezing cold night.

Just a month earlier a man in a nearby village had committed suicide by going into a field, drinking a bottle of whisky, or as much of it as he could get down him, and lying down on the grass in his shirt and trousers. He had died of the cold. The story had been on the

31

front page of the local paper. The man had been 98-years-old at the time and he had been suffering from Parkinson's disease.

And that, I felt sure, was what Hamilton was planning.

I now had to find him before it was too late.

No one in the village knew Hamilton better than Peter Marshall.

Hamilton did all his shopping at Peter's shop; he went there two or three times a week.

I didn't like doing it but I had no option. I swore him to secrecy and then told Peter my fear.

'Where would he go if he was planning to do anything silly?' I asked.

We always call it 'doing something silly' but it's a daft thing to say because to the person planning suicide, the action is anything but 'silly'.

Peter thought for a moment.

'He'd go somewhere on the cliffs between Combe Martin and Heddon's Mouth,' said Peter. 'That's always been his favourite part of the coast. And he loves the sea. Does he have his bike with him?'

'Yes, but not the trailer.'

'If he took his bike but left the trailer then he's planning to go on the footpath above the cliffs,' said Peter. 'I think he'd go down to Combe Martin and then up the hill to Hangman's Point and along the coast. He wouldn't go as far as Heddon's Mouth. Even at this time of the year and in this unseasonably cold weather there would probably be too many tourists there.'

I looked at my watch. It was just a few minutes shy of two o'clock. 'What time does it get dark?'

'Around half past seven,' replied Peter. 'I can tell you exactly…' he turned away, presumably intending to consult a calendar or newspaper.

'We've got no more than five hours,' I said. 'It'll be impossible to find him in the dark.

'I'll shut the shop and come with you,' said Peter immediately. I felt eternally grateful to him. Peter rarely shuts his shop in the middle of the day. He is too frightened that he might miss a sale. It was, for him, a great sacrifice.

'Thank you,' I said. 'I'm going to drive down into Combe Martin to start looking for him. You speak to as many people as you can find and get them to help. Try ringing people up first – Thumper,

Patchy, Frank and so on. Explain that Hamilton thinks he is dying but he isn't. The hospital made a mistake. Explain everything and tell them where we think he's gone. We don't have enough people and there isn't enough time to spread the effort anywhere else. We have to hope he's gone along the coastal path.'

'He will have done,' said Peter, confidently.

Hoping that he was right, I climbed back into the car and hurtled off down the lane into Combe Martin.

Thirty minutes later I was climbing the steep hill which leads from the picturesque coastal village of Combe Martin and following the coastal path which meanders along the cliffs between Hangman Point and Blackstone Point. My heart was pounding, partly from the physical effort and partly from anxiety. I was desperate to find Hamilton before he did anything I knew I would regret to the end of my life.

We all make mistakes, hospitals are no exception, but the consequences of this simple error were too awful for me to contemplate.

The cliff path is steep and rocky but you can, if you are a fit and accomplished cyclist, and your machine is sufficiently low geared, ride up most of the hill. But you travel slowly. I kept my eyes open but I did not expect to see any sign of Hamilton yet. If he had come this way he would be further along the path. And he would have probably moved off the path to find a quiet niche where he could lie down and drink his whisky.

Overhead a hawk was circling. On the ground a solitary pair of fantail doves, probably refugees from some nearby comfortable dovecote, were walking round in circles looking rather lost. There is nothing a hawk likes better than a plump, domesticated, settled, peace loving dove.

During the warm summer months the coastal path which runs along the North Devon coast is crowded with hikers and walkers. Some are carrying tents and food and are intent on walking the whole way around the coast, either heading west down into Cornwall, past Land's End, and then along the southern coast of Cornwall and Devon or heading east towards Lynton, Lynmouth and Porlock. Others, the vast majority, are just out for the day, carrying little more than a bottle of water, a candy bar and a map.

But today the path was deserted.

Very few people walk along the coastal path on freezing cold days when the ground is already frozen and there is a real possibility of snow in the air. The weather in North Devon doesn't pay much attention to the seasons.

When the weather is cold and there is a wind coming in from the south west, as there was, the cliff top is pretty well deserted. A few hardy dog walkers venture up to Hangman Point with their animals but even if they reach the top they soon turn back and head back home or to one of the village's many public houses.

I reached the top of the hill and headed east along the path which leads to Heddon's Mouth, Woody Bay, Lee Bay and then, eventually, to Lynton and Lynmouth. Normally, it is a beautiful walk, with stunning views across the Bristol Channel to the Welsh coast. But today I didn't have time to enjoy the view. I was looking for a patient, a friend and a fellow villager. I was looking for Hamilton.

Every now and then I called his name; hoping that he would hear me and respond. A lone walker, well wrapped up against the cold, passed by and asked if I was calling for a lost dog. I shook my head and told him I was looking for a friend I had lost. He said he had walked from Woody Bay but hadn't seen anyone other than a couple of young hikers on the path.

I carried on walking and calling for Hamilton. I was desperate to find him before it went dark. At night, on the cliffs, he would, as I was convinced he had planned, freeze to death. The sky was dark, heavy with rain clouds, and it seemed as though night was falling several hours early. The deteriorating weather was making our task more difficult by the minute. I was wearing just my sports jacket and flannels and I was freezing cold.

As I walked I was shouting his name; shouting my name; shouting that everything was fine; begging Hamilton to call out and tell me where he was.

Every time I saw a likely patch of rocks, I crossed over to them to check them out.

If Hamilton had already drunk all or some of the whisky he'd bought he might already be sleeping or semi-conscious; unable to hear me or, even if he heard me, unable to respond.

Suddenly, I heard the sound of a high revving engine. I turned, looked behind me and saw a motorbike scrabbling and racing along the cliff top path. I wondered who on earth could be crazy enough to do such a thing. Motorbikes are, of course, banned from the path, not just to protect the integrity of the path itself, and the safety of other walkers, but because riding a motorbike along a narrow trail just inches away from a drop of several hundred feet down onto the rocky coves of North Devon is not a particularly safe activity.

'What idiot could that be?' I asked myself, as I hurried along, constantly searching for signs of my lost patient.

'I thought this would be quicker!' I heard someone shout, above the sound of the motorbike.

I turned.

It was Patchy Fogg, my brother-in-law and local antique dealer extraordinaire. He had turned on the motorbike's headlight and the lamp shone brightly in the early gloaming. Patchy had adapted the bike himself, putting on thick, heavily studded tyres. The mudguards are suspended on long stays.

'Peter's got us a dozen people here,' said Patchy. 'He explained what's happened.'

Patchy reached behind him and patted the pillion seat. 'Jump on, this will be quicker than walking. We can cover more ground.'

'Where are all the others?'

'They're following behind. They'll spread out and cover all the land on both sides of the path.'

I climbed onto the back of Patchy's trial motorbike. I'd forgotten he had it. He doesn't often use it these days.

'I'll steer the damned thing, you keep a look out,' said Patchy. 'But hold on tight. It's a bit bumpy along here and it won't help if you get thrown off.'

I didn't need to be told twice. I put one arm round Patchy's waist and clung to him for dear life. The sky was very black and the headlight on Patchy's motor bike was now essential.

We found Hamilton fifteen minutes later, just as it was really going dark.

I spotted the front wheel of his bicycle, half hidden behind a huge rock on the cliffs overlooking Elwill Bay, just short of Trenishoe. Hamilton had settled into a grassy nook, just above the cliff edge and since he was on the left, or seaward side of the path, it was lucky that I spotted the bicycle wheel. I had been paying most of my attention to the inland side of the path. I shouted to Patchy to stop the motorbike, and leapt off the minute the bike skidded to a halt.

Hamilton was unconscious. The bottle, which he was still clutching, was three quarters empty. I wrapped my coat around him and cursorily checked him over. Apart from the fact that he was clearly drunk and semi-comatose there didn't seem to be anything wrong with him. He mumbled something but he wasn't in a fit state to understand anything. He was cold, very cold. Alcohol dilates the blood vessels and exacerbates normal heat loss.

'Ride back along the path,' I told Patchy. 'I can't carry him and we can't put him on your bike but two of us can carry him between us. Tell anyone you see that we've found Hamilton and we need help.'

Five minutes later, Patchy came roaring back along the path with Thumper riding pillion. As Thumper jumped off, Patchy sped back along the track.

'You and I will carry him for as far as we can,' said Thumper. 'Then Patchy will bring more help on his bike.'

Hamilton was too drunk to walk, too incapable to put one foot in front of the other with any hope or expectation that the result would be a move in the required direction. So Thumper and I lifted him together and carried him between us.

While I'd been waiting for help, I'd hidden Hamilton's bicycle more effectively behind the rocks. It would be safe enough until the next morning. It was quite dark now and difficult to see where we were walking. The rain had started and, blown by the wind, it was sharp and stinging. Thumper and I stumbled along the path, cursing whenever we caught a foot on a fixed stone.

After another five minutes, Patchy appeared again. This time he had Peter Marshall riding pillion. And so we managed a sort of impromptu rota system, carrying Hamilton bit by bit, yard by yard, along the coast path. From time to time, I checked his pulse. It was fine.

When we got to Combe Martin we put Hamilton into the back of the Rolls Royce and took him to the cottage hospital in Bilbury. I didn't want to take him all the way to Barnstaple. Besides, suicide had been illegal in England until just a few years earlier and I thought it best that we keep the knowledge of what had happened to ourselves. When something like this happens in Bilbury then we make sure that it stays in Bilbury. We are a village where we like to look after one another and we don't like having to risk other people making judgements.

Officially, and for administrative reasons, our village hospital is known as the Brownlow County Hotel. But in reality it is an excellent cottage hospital. We undressed Hamilton and put him into bed. I stayed with him until he woke a couple of hours later. By that time Patchy had ridden back along the path, taking Thumper with him, and the two of them had retrieved Hamilton's bicycle. Patchy knew that Hamilton would worry about it.

'The hospital made a mistake,' I told him. 'Your X-ray is clear. You don't have cancer. You're not dying.' I struggled hard, and failed, to stop myself shivering. I was still soaked to the skin because I hadn't been able to go back to Bilbury Grange for fresh, dry clothes.

Hamilton stared at me for a moment and then nodded his understanding.

'I'm so terribly sorry,' I said. I was soaked but I was very, very happy.

'Not your fault,' said Hamilton. He looked at me, frowned and thought for a moment. 'Where's my bicycle?'

'Back at your cottage,' I told him. 'Patchy Fogg and Thumper Robinson collected it and took it back home.'

'Good,' said Hamilton. 'If that had gone missing I wouldn't have forgiven you. That would have been your fault.'

I smiled at him and nodded.

'I know,' I said.

'Tickety tonk,' he said, with the beginnings of a grin. And then he closed his eyes and went back to sleep.

Hamilton was going to be absolutely fine.

Blue Peter

'On a cold day 90% of body heat is lost through the head,' said Peter Marshall, suddenly and without provocation or encouragement.

Peter, Thumper Robinson, Patchy Fogg and I were sitting in the snug at the Duck and Puddle.

Englishmen have enjoyed good companionship in public houses since the days of the Mermaid Tavern in London in the 17th century. Regulars there included Sir Walter Ralegh, John Donne and William Shakespeare. I'm prepared to admit that their conversation was probably slightly more sophisticated than ours, but the principle is the same. As, indeed, it has been for centuries.

After the Mermaid Tavern came the London coffee houses, as favoured by Dr Samuel Johnson. Then came the coffee houses of Vienna and Paris and, in the 20th century, meeting places such as the Round Table at the Algonquin Hotel in New York. Thus it always was and, hopefully, always ever will be.

It was lunchtime, or, to be honest, a little after lunchtime. We had been discussing what makes a gentleman. Outside, temporarily escaping from the cold, a pair of companionable wood pigeons were sitting on a branch directly above the chimney from the Duck and Puddle's ancient boiler. The boiler is situated in one of the Duck and Puddle's rickety out buildings and works only when the fancy takes it. The fancy had clearly taken it for it was working.

The pigeons were clearly enjoying the rising smoke and would occasionally lift a wing so as to take full advantage of the warm air. The boiler provides occasional hot water for washing and bathing and heats a few radiators upstairs so that the pub's occasional guests don't freeze to death. Downstairs, the public and private rooms in the pub are heated by log fires.

Predictably, Peter Marshall said that a gentleman is a fellow who always pays his bills on time and preferably in cash. Thumper mentioned the fact that Peter had frequently expressed a reluctance to pay his income tax bills on time and Peter responded, not unreasonably we all thought, by pointing out that giving money to governments of any hue is sinful and should be illegal. 'The money they are given is invariably spent and always wasted,' he said. 'They use it to start wars, oppress the indigent and treat themselves to endless slap up dinners and bottles of expensive claret.'

No one could find fault in this and we all agreed that in view of all the bad things politicians do with the money we give them, it would make sense for the Government to punish tax payers and give honours and medals to those upstanding citizens who refuse to contribute to war mongering and oppression.

Bringing the subject of bill paying closer to home, I pointed out to Peter that he still owed Patsy and me a very ungentlemanly £22 for three peck of apples and a bushel of potatoes which we had supplied to his shop a couple of years back, in 1971. Peter responded, predictably I suppose, by pointing out that he had never claimed to be a gentleman and that if indeed he did owe us any money he would render payment if we resubmitted an appropriate invoice.

(Regardless of what the rest of the country does, or may do in the future, we still use old-fashioned imperial measurements in Bilbury. We live by pounds and ounces and feet and inches and pecks and bushels and, however much the bureaucrats may huff and puff, those fiddly metric things they favour on the continent of Europe will never find favour in our part of North Devon. Men in suits, carrying clipboards, are rarer than Montagu's harrier in our part of the world.)

Thumper said that in his view, a gentleman was someone who always put an old cloth on top of the kitchen table before working on bits of his truck engine. He said that his good lady, Anne Thwaites, always said that it was the one thing which had convinced her that underneath his rough exterior lay the heart, soul and spirit of an English gentleman.

It was agreed by the company present that putting a cloth on the table before working on parts of your truck engine was a pretty gentlemanly thing to do.

And then Patchy said that he had heard that a gentleman was a fellow who if he opened the door to a bathroom and saw a lady in the tub, would back out, close the door, and say 'Excuse me, sir, sorry to have bothered you.'

We all laughed and agreed that Patchy's definition pretty well finished that particular discussion.

'Talking of people coming into the bathroom,' Patchy continued, 'reminds me that Adrienne came into the bathroom this morning and asked if I knew I had a bald patch.'

Adrienne, his wife, is my sister-in-law and a graduate with honours from the Captain Bligh School of Diplomacy'. She is not known for her tact. In the unlikely event that she ever becomes Foreign Secretary we will, within weeks, be at war with every other country on the planet.

Thumper stood up so that he could look down on Patchy's head. 'She's right,' he said. 'But, never mind, your hair probably just lost its way.'

'What do you mean, it lost its way?' demanded Patchy.

'Well, it's growing out of your ears now,' explained Thumper.

Patchy stuck a finger in each ear in turn. 'I can't feel any hair there.'

'There is,' said Thumper.

'He's right,' said Peter. 'You need to get one of those electrical gadgets for cutting ear hair.'

'I don't suppose you've got some for sale, have you?' said Patchy.

'Oddly enough I had some come in the other day,' said Peter. 'Brilliant value. Guaranteed to get rid of ear and nose hair in seconds.' Peter always has something to sell to everyone.

Patchy did not look particularly excited by Peter's remarks about ear and nose hair. He has not, I suspect, been properly prepared for the many tricks fate plays on the maturing male.

We all sat in silence for a few moments, contemplating our ageing bodies. Baldness, deafness, deteriorating eyesight, liver spots and worse all beckoned.

Gloomily, I glanced out of the window and watched a seagull stamping on a stretch of grass in the hope of convincing a worm that it was raining and that he should emerge from his lair. As the seagull stamped, it moved slowly backwards. For a moment I wondered why it was going in reverse, and then I realised that if it went forwards it wouldn't see any of the worms which its stamping had tricked into emerging.

I didn't mention this to anyone because I found it slightly embarrassing to realise that I had come second to a seagull in a simple intelligence test.

Twenty minutes earlier we had all finished vast platefuls of Gilly's vegetable soup (so rich it is a meal in itself) and had mopped up our plates with thick slices cut from one of her home-made farmhouse loaves. Frank, who is a huge fan of his wife's cooking (and, despite having lost a good deal of weight recently, still has the waistline to prove it) always says that if you've never eaten one of Gilly's home-made farmhouse loaves then you have never tasted bread as God intended it to taste.

The soup is named 'Thumper's Bellyfiller', in recognition of my dear friend Thumper Robinson, who is renowned throughout North Devon for having a trencherman's appetite. Even Thumper admits that he cannot possibly eat more than one bowlful of the stuff.

Gilly is constantly looking for ways to enhance the appeal of the Duck and Puddle and she has taken to naming several of the dishes on the pub's menu after local citizens. There is a dish involving three slices of toast and four scrambled eggs which is named after her husband, Frank, and a four sausage version of Toad in the Hole which is named after Patchy Fogg. My own name is immortalised in the form of a version of treacle pudding of which I am unreasonably fond.

Peter then took advantage of the momentary silence to try to sell us all one of his new thermally insulated Chapeau Watch Caps. He told us he had bought a consignment from a wholesaler who had, in turn, purchased the entire stock from a Canadian manufacturer who had gone bankrupt. Peter always has something to sell. Just the other day I noticed that he was selling leftover hazelnuts, unsold after Christmas, with the promotional slogan 'Grow Your Own Kindling' stencilled on a piece of brown cardboard torn from a delivery box. When I queried this, Peter pointed out that hazel grows very quickly and that within ten years of planting there would be kindling to harvest.

'They're wind-proof and rain-proof and they absorb the sun's rays, thereby protecting the head in all weathers,' Peter said, describing his hats with great enthusiasm and drifting automatically into patter mode. 'I'm selling them at lower than retail price as a service to the village.'

If Peter specialises in anything it is in buying bankrupt stock.

He would think himself in nirvana if he could buy cheese and milk from a bankrupt farmer, bread from a bankrupt baker and apples from a bankrupt fruit grower.

The watch caps, which apparently came in a curious shade of dark purple (without the option) were, Peter told us, with the unfettered enthusiasm of a man in search of a profit, guaranteed to fit any head and to keep it warmer than any other headgear.

Hats for men are going out of fashion rapidly and I fear that by the start of the 1980's they will be remembered as nothing more than a historical oddity. They were, however, once a sign of a man's status, individuality and fashion sense. Would Napoleon have conquered Europe if he had worn a woolly hat with a bobble on the top? Would Wellington have won at Waterloo if he'd favoured one of those deerstalker hats, complete with ear flaps, favoured by costume directors dressing up an actor to play Sherlock Holmes? Would Abraham Lincoln have been Abraham Lincoln if he'd worn a blue beret?

I was, I admit, tempted by one of Peter's watch caps for the winds in North Devon can be ferocious. They come, predominantly, from the South West and they scour the cliffs and heathland with unremitting, unforgiving anger; seemingly determined to remove every last shred of vegetation or habitation from the county.

I have found, by experience, that when you live in an area heavily populated by seagulls it is wise to wear a hat whenever possible. I have a rather nice tweed fishing hat, a soft slouch hat and a couple of rather splendid pieces of headgear, both made by Bates, a hatter who has a shop in Jermyn Street in London. One of my hats, known as a Grosvenor, was bought for the winter and the other, a Panama, for the summer.

I do not favour cloth caps of the style favoured by the politician Keir Hardie. It is difficult to persuade a stranger to have faith in you as a doctor if you turn up looking like an off duty bookmaker. Baseball caps, which are now beginning to find much favour, are excellent at providing shade for the eyes but seem more suited to a younger head. And nor, generally speaking, do I favour woolly hats. They are fine for walkers and hikers but it is impossible to look dignified, wise or even adequately competent if you are wearing a woolly hat, especially if it has an attached bobble bouncing around.

But the winds of North Devon are no respecter of seasons and there is, more often than not, a wind capable of removing almost any hat from almost any head. It occurred to me that a watch cap, tightly fitting and with no parts likely to catch the wind, might be persuaded to stay in situ on even the stormiest of days.

'The human body loses 90% of its heat through the head,' insisted Peter again, with all the definitive confidence of a man who has read something somewhere, and who has a vested interest in it being accepted as the truth.

'How on earth do you know that?' asked Thumper who is not normally a sceptical man but who is always prepared to give Peter the sticky end of the doubt.

'I read it,' said Peter. 'In a book,' he added, in the clear understanding that he felt that this would give the assertion added gravitas.

'You've never read a book in your life,' said Patchy with a laugh.

'I did,' responded Peter indignantly. 'I read one of those books on the table in the hairdressers.'

Peter lets out an old shed to a variety of local businesses. The hairdresser is one of the businesses renting the shed. And, inevitably, on the days when hair is being snipped, a rickety old table is piled high with tatty, old magazines.

'Those are magazines not books,' Thumper pointed out.

'Well I read it in one of those,' said Peter, defiantly. He looked around, defying us to contradict the power of the printed word. 'So it must be true. It was written by a doctor and you can't argue with medical science.' He looked at me when he said this, defying me to argue with medical science.

I kept quiet. I find it is far more fun to allow Peter's assertions to explore their limits.

'So if you went outside on a cold day and you wore nothing but one of your hats you'd still be quite warm?' said Thumper.

'You'd lose a little bit of heat,' said Peter.

'Ten per cent,' said Patchy.

Peter looked at him.

'That's what left when you take 90% from 100%,' Patchy explained. 'You said that the body loses 90% of its heat through the head.'

'Exactly!' said Peter, with a nod. 'Ten per cent.'

'It's pretty cold today,' said Thumper.

'Freezing,' said Patchy. 'Unseasonably chilly.'

We all looked out of the window.

The road outside the Duck and Puddle had been white with frost that morning. And the hills in the distance were still white. The sun was shining, but up on the higher fields and moorland the temperature still wasn't warm enough to melt the frost. It was, in truth, unseasonably cold and Bilbury looked very Christmassy.

'So are you going to prove it?' asked Thumper.

'Do an experiment,' suggested Patchy.

Peter looked at them. 'What do you mean?'

'Take your clothes off and go outside in just a hat,' said Patchy. 'See if you stay warm.'

Peter looked out of the window at the white on the distant hills.

It was very warm in the snug at the Duck and Puddle. Frank had lit a log fire, built with well dried logs from one of the dead apple trees Patsy's father had cut down in his orchard. The fire was crackling and comforting. Central heating is all very well but it only keeps you warm. A log fire provides visual and auditory delights as well as keeping you warm.

'Have you got one of your hats with you?' asked Thumper.

'One of the Chapeau Watch Caps,' said Patchy.

'I came in one,' said Peter proudly, pulling a hat from his jacket pocket. Except for the colour, which was, as advertised, a unique shade of purple, it looked pretty much like any other woolly hat.

'I'll buy one if you really can stay warm wearing nothing else,' I told Peter. I took the hat from him and examined it. 'Are you sure you don't have any other colours?' I asked, before handing the hat back to him.

It was, in truth, a rather sorry looking thing but I thought it would serve as suitable headgear for working in the garden.

'This is the only colour,' said Peter. 'It's next year's fashionable colour.'

Peter's idea of 'what is in fashion' is exactly the same as 'what he can buy cheaply because no one else wants it'.

Thumper and Patchy, who have never knowingly worn anything fashionable, except by accident, promised that they too would buy hats if Peter's experiment proved successful.

'If I wear one of these hats will I be able to play tennis?' asked Patchy.

'Oh yes,' said Peter instantly.

'That's terrific,' said Patchy drily. 'I've always wanted to be able to play tennis.'

Peter sucked his teeth and tried to smile.

'Right,' said Thumper. 'Strip off and pop outside for half an hour.'

'Half an hour?' said Peter. 'What am I going to do for half an hour?'

'Shiver?' suggested Patchy.

'Just stand there being warm and cosy,' I suggested. 'Proving that your Chapeau Watch Cap keeps you warm. And while you're out there you can look forward to selling three hats when you come inside.'

It was cold outside but it wasn't cold enough to do him any harm. And since Peter rips us all off mercilessly we feel obliged, from time to time, to have a little fun at his expense.

Peter stood up and removed his jacket. It is sometimes said that everyone has a little touch of genius hidden inside them. If this is true then Peter's genius is his ability to demean himself in any way necessary if doing so might help him make a profit. He would swim naked through a pool full of piranha fish in order to sell a can of beans or a box of matches. It is the Peter we all know and sort of love. I wouldn't have him any other way.

'How much do I have to take off?'

'Everything,' said Thumper. 'It's the only way to do the experiment.'

'If you're going to do it then you might as well do it properly,' I said.

Peter removed his shoes, his socks, his trousers, his shirt and a grey string vest. We allowed him to keep his underpants on. They too were grey. None of us felt we could cope with the consequences of his removing them. I couldn't help admiring his socks which had been darned many times by someone (probably Peter himself) using odds and ends of coloured wool.

I couldn't help wondering whether people will still be darning socks in a few decades time. It seemed more than likely that socks with holes in them will simply be discarded and replaced. We are

45

developing into a 'throw-away' society. When I was a boy the word 'thrifty' was used as a compliment. Today it is used in a rather critical, almost derisory, way.

'You must stay in view,' said Thumper. 'Go outside and stand by the window so that we can see you.'

'If you turn blue we'll call off the experiment and come and fetch you,' I told him. 'We don't want you to die for a hat.'

'I'll be as warm as toast,' insisted Peter. He sounded defiant and confident but I know him well enough to know that an element of doubt had crept into the forefront of his mind.

Two minutes later Peter was standing on the forecourt outside the Duck and Puddle. We could see him clearly from where we were sitting.

'Shall we order another round?' suggested Patchy.

'Good idea,' said Thumper. He called for Frank.

'What'll be?' asked the landlord.

'Three hot whiskies,' said Thumper. He looked round. Patchy and I both nodded. There's nothing more comforting than a hot whisky when you're watching a fellow human being shivering in the cold.

'Where's Peter?' asked Frank.

We all looked to the window.

'What the blazes is Peter doing outside?' asked Frank. He walked closer to the window. 'Why is he naked?' he asked, shocked and horrified in equal proportions.

'He isn't quite naked,' said Patchy.

'He's wearing a hat and his underpants,' I pointed out.

'It's an experiment,' explained Thumper. 'Peter says that a human being loses 90% of his body heat through his head. So he's proving that he can stand outside in the frost and stay warm while wearing nothing but a hat.'

'I've not had so much fun since I had measles,' said Patchy, staring out of the window.

Frank looked at us, one by one. 'Is he mad? Or am I mad?'

We looked at him but none of us said anything. There are some questions which don't need to be answered.

'Silly question,' said Frank with a sigh. 'I'll get the whiskies.'

Three minutes later he returned with a tray upon which were standing three Russian tea glasses, each one containing a generous portion of malt whisky, and a jug of hot water.

'I'll let you add your own hot water,' he said, putting the tray down on our table.

'Why is Peter standing on our forecourt wearing only a woolly hat and a nasty looking pair of baggy underpants?' asked Gilly, Frank's wife, who had accompanied him back into the snug.

'It's an experiment,' explained Frank.

'Oh,' said Gilly, apparently satisfied by this explanation. 'Is he going to be there long? It's just that I don't think he's much of an attraction for the passing trade.'

'Do you get much passing trade at this time of year?' asked Patchy.

'None whatsoever,' admitted Gilly. 'The hikers and walkers stop hiking and walking when the weather gets cold.'

'Wise folk,' said Thumper.

'He's jumping up and down,' said Frank.

We looked out of the window. Peter was indeed now jumping up and down.

'We did stuff like that when I did my National Service,' said Frank. 'We had to go outside in our shorts and do jumping up and down exercises. I think they thought that if we ran out of ammunition we could do it to scare the Germans.'

'Sounds like a good strategy to me,' said Thumper. 'The Germans would have run a mile if they'd seen you jumping up and down in a pair of shorts.'

'Shrivels up the essential bits,' said Frank. 'Everyone went into the showers with their hands over their parts after we'd done star jumps in the snow.'

Gilly looked at him and raised an eyebrow but said nothing.

'Was he that colour when he went outside?' asked Thumper, nodding in Peter's direction.

'I don't think that is a natural colour for a human being,' said Patchy.

'They're usually dead when they're that colour,' I said.

Thumper poured a little water into his whisky. Patchy and I followed suit.

'I think I'll join you,' said Frank.

'That'll be your daily ration,' Gilly said to him sternly. 'And bring the bottle so that I can pour.'

47

Gilly understands Frank. And as Frank himself admits she has been an angel as well as a wife. Frank had a stroke a few months earlier and Gilly was keeping an eye on his eating and drinking in order to keep his blood pressure under control.

'OK dear,' said Frank meekly. He sounded disappointed but resigned to his fate. 'But the doc's here,' he added, as though that made a difference.

'I'll pour,' repeated Gilly firmly.

Frank went off and returned moments later with another glass and the bottle of Laphroaig.

'He's changed colour again,' said Patchy.

We all looked out of the window once more.

'He's still alive anyway,' said Patchy. 'He's moving a bit.'

Peter had gone from pink to white. If you'd stuck three pieces of coal in a row down his chest he'd have been a dead ringer for a snowman.

'I'd better go and fetch him,' I said, not wanting to wait until he suffered frost bite. He had only been outside for about ten minutes but Peter is not a man for whom the word 'fortitude' was invented. He looked pretty miserable. I took a sip from my hot whisky and then turned to Frank. 'You'd better get him a glass,' I said. 'I think Peter will need something to warm up his cockles.'

'Is that what they're called?' said Gilly, smirking. She had acquired a glass of her own. She doesn't drink whisky. Her glass contained hot, mulled red wine. As I walked past her I could smell the nutmeg and the cloves. If I hadn't been drinking hot Laphroaig I'd have been envious.

'You'd better come in,' I said to Peter, from the pub's front doorway. 'You look a bit on the chilly side.'

'I'm as w-w-w-warm as I w-w-w-would be if I'd h-h-h-had m-m-m-my c-c-c-clothes on,' he stuttered.

I realised at that point that our experiment had been not well designed since it made no allowance for cheating on the part of the experimental subject.

Peter, moving gingerly, as befits a man with frozen limbs and bits and pieces, moved as rapidly as was possible and headed towards me. His teeth were chattering.

'I n-n-n-need the loo!' he whispered.

It was no doubt the cold. Men of Peter's age need the loo every two hours and every twenty minutes in cold weather. (In contrast, women can hold out for a day or two but they then take an hour to empty their bladder so the procedures pretty much even out.)

I waited for Peter. He emerged from the Gents a few minutes later and then followed me into the bar. He was still shivering.

'Put your clothes on,' said Thumper. 'I can't drink whisky sitting next to a man in those underpants.'

But Peter's fingers were too cold to do anything involving buttons. Gilly, the most thoughtful landlady in any public house in Britain, found him a blanket and wrapped it around him.

'I don't think the hat was big enough,' said Patchy.

Peter opened his mouth to speak but his teeth were now chattering too much for words to escape unhindered.

'I can tell you the problem,' said Frank. 'There's no bobble on the hat.'

'I think there was a bobble when he went out,' said Patchy. 'But it's shrivelled up in the cold.'

Peter, who looked very miserable, pulled the blanket round him and moved to a chair nearer to the fire.

'Don't sit too close to the fire or you'll get chilblains,' warned Thumper, who had clearly been taught about such things by someone who believed that sitting on cold stones causes piles and that you can't get pregnant if you do it standing up.

'Can you get chilblains on your bits and pieces?' asked Patchy.

'Only on your feet,' said Frank, as though he knew what he was talking about. 'And that's rubbish about sitting near to the fire. You just get them if you get cold. If any part of your body becomes too cold it'll just drop off. The blood supply stops and the next thing you know your bits are all lying on the floor. I read that somewhere.'

'Actually you can get chilblains on all sorts of extremities,' I said quietly, thinking that I perhaps ought to add a little real science to the conversation. 'Fingers, toes…' I paused, leaving the rest to the imagination.

Thumper and Patchy both shivered at the unspoken thought.

Peter cautiously opened the blanket and looked inside his underpants. When he closed the blanket again he seemed relieved.

'What about frostbite?' asked Patchy. 'I remember reading one of those books about explorers walking across the Antarctic and the author said that if you get too cold your toes and fingers are likely to fall off.'

'You'd better stand on the rug,' said Frank to Peter.

Peter looked at him, puzzled.

'In case any of your toes fall off,' explained Frank. 'There are big gaps between our floorboards. We don't want your toes falling down into the cellar. It'll take ages to find them down there.' He paused. 'And I'm not entirely sure that there aren't some little creatures living among the barrels,' he added.

Peter shuddered and leapt onto the safety of the rug. He then looked down at his toes which were now regaining a little of their natural colour.

We sipped our drinks and watched Peter shiver. I suppose it was very irresponsible of us to have let him get so cold but it was Peter after all. Peter is pretty well indestructible. And no one had forced him to stay outside.

'I think we can safely say that the experiment was a failure,' said Patchy.

'Well, it wasn't really a failure,' I pointed out. 'It simply proved that Peter was sort of wrong. You can't keep warm wearing nothing but a hat and a pair of ropey old underpants.'

'So much for medical science,' said Patchy.

'Everything I've got is painful and itchy,' complained Peter, standing up and rubbing his hands over his body.

'You've got frostnip,' I told him. 'Everything is painful and itchy because you're warming up.'

'Will he live?' asked Frank.

'He'll live,' I told him. 'No one ever died of frostnip.'

Peter, at least, looked relieved.

'I'm definitely going to buy one of Peter's hats anyway,' said Thumper. 'As a memento of the day.'

Patchy, Frank and I confirmed that we'd all buy one too. I think we all felt sorry for Peter and wanted to cheer him up. But Patchy, the only true businessman among us, insisted that we would only buy the hats if, as bulk buyers, we were all given a decent discount.

Peter, who had suddenly and miraculously recovered from his bout of frostnip and had perked up considerably, immediately offered us a measly 5% discount. Patchy demanded 10%. They settled for 7.5%.

Despite the modest discount (usually something which always causes him great distress), the sale of four of his hats cheered Peter up considerably.

'I'll pop to the shop and get them now that I've warmed up a bit,' he promised, probably unwilling to wait too long in case we changed our minds.

'Then we'd better stay here a bit longer,' said Thumper. 'And wait for you to get back.'

'It's a hard life,' I said, sipping at my malt. I looked at my watch. There was plenty of time before evening surgery was due to start. Patsy had gone into Barnstaple with her sister but Miss Johnson knew where I was and would ring the Duck and Puddle if there were any calls for me.

'Someone's got to live it,' said Patchy, with a sigh.

'Might as well be us,' said Thumper.

'Without you lot Frank and I wouldn't have any customers in the winter,' said Gilly, with disarming honesty.

'I suppose we'd better have another round of hot whiskies,' said Thumper.

'Jolly good idea,' said Frank. 'I'll put another log on the fire when I've poured the whiskies.'

'You can have hot lemonade,' said Gilly to her husband. 'You've had your alcohol allowance for the day.

To my surprise and delight Frank did not say a word in protest. I was proud of him. I quietly wished that all my patients were as sensible, and had such loving and determined spouses.

Then, as we sat and waited for Peter to return. Thumper said he was glad that he was buying one of the hats Peter was selling because now he'd have something to give me for Christmas. I told him it was funny that he'd said that because I had similar plans for the hat I was buying.

That took us onto talking about presents and Patchy said that a cousin of his, who was not a romantic man, once told his wife that he was giving her 'something for her pretty neck' for Christmas. The wife, who was expecting a string of pearls, or a pretty necklace of some kind, was heartily disappointed when she received a box containing two bars of soap. Patchy said that his cousin told him that for three months, bedroom activity fell away to the sort of level common in the more strictly run monasteries and nunneries.

Thumper said he'd learned his lesson about presents several years earlier when he'd given his good lady, Anne, a two-speed hammer drill for Christmas. He realised that he hadn't been as clever as he'd thought he'd been when she gave him a pair of hair curling tongs for his birthday three months later.

Just then Peter returned with our hats. We all tried them on and agreed that we looked pretty much like a bunch of Alaskan crabbers on shore leave.

Patchy said he would give his hat to Thumper for Christmas. Frank said he rather liked his hat and that he would give it to Gilly so that she could give it to him for Christmas. Gilly said that if she got one for Christmas she would hit the giver over the head with a saucepan as a 'thank you'.

Peter, who doesn't believe in giving presents or sending cards but who is not averse to receiving either or both, and who regularly encourages his customers to buy and send gifts and cards at every possible opportunity, said he hadn't thought of the Chapeau Watch Cap headgear as suitable to be sold as Christmas presents but that since we'd all indicated that the hats had 'present potential' he would prepare a window display with half a dozen of the hats decorated with a piece of tinsel which he'd found in a cupboard.

'Christmas is months away!' Frank pointed out.

'You can never be too early to take advantage of the Christmas rush,' said Peter.

It was April.

Surprise, surprise!

Carole and Gordon Singer had been married for years, and I had always thought of them as a loving couple. But they came to see me separately.

And they both had strange stories to tell.

Their stories were very different but although they were different they were also the same.

'About a year ago, Carole told me she wanted to start going to an exercise class,' began Gordon. 'She started off by just going to a class on Friday evenings. It was held in Barnstaple because there is nothing like that in Bilbury. But after a few weeks, she said she felt so much better for it that she thought she'd go to a class on Saturday lunchtimes as well.'

'I thought she looked good when I last saw her,' I said. 'She's lost some weight.'

'She's lost half a stone,' agreed Gordon. 'And she looks marvellous. She's thirty nine next birthday but you'd never guess. She's always made a real effort to look good but in the last year or two she seems to have really put in an effort to keep her figure. I think she's got a wonderful figure but she always says she thinks her bum is too big' He paused, thinking. 'But most women seem to think their bum is too big, don't they?'

He was clearly proud of his wife but there was also a strange sort of sadness in the way he spoke; and that rather surprised me for I didn't understand where the sadness was coming from. Why would a man be proud and pleased that his wife was still making an effort to look good but at the same time be sad about it?

And then I realised.

Maybe, Gordon had found out that Carole was having an affair. Or maybe he suspected that she might be having an affair.

I was, at that moment, beginning to think that this story had the makings of a family tragedy.

'I only found out the truth by accident,' said Gordon. He shuffled about on the chair for a moment or two, as people often do when they aren't quite sure how to proceed with the conversation, and they want to delay things for as long as possible.

I waited.

There is no point in hurrying people when they want to tell you something but they don't really want to talk about it. If you try to rush things then they tell you something else, usually of little consequence, and leave the important things unsaid.

'I don't much like being in the house on my own,' said Gordon when he was finally comfortable, 'and so once or twice recently I've met up with a few pals for a drink. We usually go somewhere local – the Duck and Puddle, the Old Station House Inn at Blackmoor Gate or the House of Cards in Combe Martin. But last week, a group of us went to a pub in Barnstaple, a place called the Gravedigger's Rest. Do you know it?'

I shook my head. I knew the other three pubs he'd mentioned, of course. But I didn't know the Gravedigger's Rest in Barnstaple. It's a popular name for pubs in North Devon. I suspect that there must have been a good many tired gravediggers in our part of the world.

'A bloke I've known for years was having a sort of stag do. He's getting married for the third time but he still wanted a bit of a party. Anyway, he wanted to go to the Gravedigger's Rest because they had a couple of strippers advertised and he thought it would be a laugh. To be honest, that sort of thing is not really my cup of tea, actually to tell you the truth I've never even been to a strip club, not a live show, but I went along just to be sociable and to have a laugh and because I didn't have anything else to do – with Carole being out at her exercise class.'

At this point I thought I knew what was coming next. I thought he was going to tell me that while he was sitting there, watching the strip show, his wife had walked in for a drink after her exercise class. And that she'd been accompanied by a man. The class instructor, perhaps. That, I thought, was going to be his story.

I tried to work out what I should say to him.

But as Gordon continued I soon realised that my supposition was absolutely, 100% wrong and that the not very wise words I'd already begun to put together were entirely useless.

'To cut a long story short, my wife was the second stripper,' said Gordon.

I managed an 'Ah' and an 'I see' but that was the extent of my contribution at this revelation. And I was quite proud that I'd managed that much.

My first thought was that I had never thought of Carole Singer as the sort of woman who would work as a stripper.

My second thought, proved entirely accurate by the facts, was that I had no idea what I had meant by that thought.

What, after all, was the stripping sort of woman?

'She was very good at it,' said Gordon. 'Fortunately, I was sitting at the back of the pub so I'm pretty sure she didn't see me. When I saw her I sort of crouched down behind a couple of rowdy big blokes who were sitting directly in front of me.'

'It must have been quite a surprise,' I said.

'You can say that again,' said Gordon.

I didn't.

'She came on in a see-through blouse and a sort of flouncy skirt which I'd never seen before and a pair of red high heeled shoes. She was wearing a curly blonde wig. There was some music being played on a tape machine and she did the bump and grind act that strippers always do in films and stripped off the skirt and the blouse and the blokes in front of me were jumping up and shouting and there was a lot of cheering and the usual sort of comments being made. She was wearing a black bra, a suspender belt and stockings and a pair of very tiny panties, one of those G-strings, less material than you'd need to make a yard of dental floss, so thin and flimsy that to be honest it was difficult to be sure whether she wearing anything at all, especially because the thing she was almost wearing was flesh coloured and almost invisible. I have to admit she looked pretty good. She's quite short as you know, only a tad over five foot tall, but she's very curvy and I got the impression that the customers in that pub liked their strippers to have a bit of meat on them; a bit curvy I suppose you might say; decent breasts and hips if you know what I mean. It wasn't difficult to see why the blokes in the pub were all egging her on. She took off the bra, wiggled her bosom about, kicked off the shoes and then peeled off the stockings until all she was wearing was the G-string. It was all done very slowly to the usual sort of musical accompaniment – provided by a tape recorder. I couldn't help noticing that she'd trimmed her pubic hair quite short; very short, actually. I hadn't noticed that before. Then she pranced around pretty well stark naked for a few minutes, weaving in and out of the blokes at the front of the crowd and trying to dodge their groping hands – not always successfully if the truth be told. I saw one bloke grab her bum and another one managed a good squeeze of one of her breasts before she wriggled away from him. She slapped his face but not too hard; just sort of letting him know he'd gone a bit too far. The other blokes laughed at him and gave him a bit of a ribbing. It was all fairly good natured.'

'Did any of the blokes you were with recognise her?' I asked him.

I felt I was swimming in a rough sea, well out of my depth and out of sight of land.

If, when I'd been at medical school, there had ever been a course on what doctors should say to husbands who have found out that their wives are taking their clothes off in public houses then I must have missed it.

'I thought one of them might have. He looked at me a bit quizzical but didn't say anything. The wig made her look quite different so I think he probably just thought it was some bird who looked a bit like Carole.'

'Then what happened?'

'She was looking out into the crowd, smiling and waving when she suddenly stopped, turned round, bent down and picked up her clothes and then darted back out through a door at the back of the pub. She didn't come back out again. A bit later there was another girl who stripped and did an act with a snake. I'm probably biased but I didn't think she was half as good as Carole. She was much younger, no more than 19 or 20 I'd say, and one of the lads said she'd had that stuff injected into her breasts to make them bigger. They certainly didn't look very realistic.' He shuddered. 'I can't stand snakes anyway. I can't even bear to pick up a grass snake.'

'So you think she might have seen you?'

'She might have. I can't be sure.'

'Have you said anything to Carole?'

'Good heavens, no! What on earth would I say?'

'You're going to have to talk about it sometime,' I told him. 'Otherwise, she'll be going out of the house telling you that she's going to her aerobics class and you'll know that she's going to a pub to take off all her clothes.'

Gordon nodded. 'I wouldn't mind so much if she hadn't lied to me about what she was doing,' he said. 'Now I'm not sure what else she's getting up to.'

'You're wondering if she's been unfaithful?'

'Well, I don't know how these things work,' said Gordon. 'But do these strippers sleep with the customers? Is she taking one or two of the blokes up into a back room after the show?'

'Oh, I'm sure she isn't,' I said, though I don't know why I'd said this. Half an hour earlier I would have probably sworn on oath that Carole Singer wasn't the sort of woman who would take her clothes off in public; appearing in a strip show in a public house. I suddenly realised that as much as I thought I knew my patients there was probably a good deal about them that I really didn't know; and would probably never know. It was quite a revelation; like having a professional cold shower.

'If it's just the stripping she does, and if she'd talked to me about it, and if it is something she really wants to do, then I wouldn't object,' said Gordon suddenly. 'She looked so alive when I saw her taking her things off. I know her well enough to know that she was clearly enjoying the attention she was getting; having all those men staring at her body. I suppose it made her feel good about herself. It would, wouldn't it?' He cleared his throat. 'She was very good at the stripping,' he said. 'She was much better than the other girl they had. And the funny thing is that I was very proud of her; proud that she could do it and proud that she was good at it. And, to be honest, I felt proud to be married to her. I think anyone would be proud to be married to her. She looks terrific. All those blokes would have been green with envy if they'd known I was married to her.'

'I'm sure,' I agreed.

I wondered if Carole was, perhaps, going through some sort of premature mid-life crisis. Maybe she no longer felt attractive. Could it be that she felt that Gordon was no longer giving her enough attention? I had suddenly found myself in the position of an agony aunt rather than a family doctor.

'So, what should I do?' asked Gordon. 'Should I tell her that I know where she goes?' He swallowed hard. 'And ask her what else she gets up to?'

'Let me think about it for a day,' I told him. 'Come back and see me this time tomorrow.'

'Do you think they get paid?'

I looked at him.

'The strippers,' he said. 'Do you think they get paid?'

'I'm sure they do,' I said. 'It's a profession isn't it? There will be expenses. Special clothes. Petrol. The girl who has the snake will have to feed it.'

'I wonder how much,' said Gordon, to himself more than to me.

'I'll think about what you've told me,' I told him again. 'Come and see me tomorrow morning.'

Gordon said he could wait another day before deciding what to do. And so off he went.

After he had gone, I sat there silent and alone for so long that Miss Johnson knocked on my consulting room door to see if I was all right.

I was still puzzling over what to say to Gordon several hours later when it was time to start the evening surgery.

And the first patient who came into the surgery was Carole Singer.

She was wearing a calf length grey tweed skirt, a grey woollen jumper and a dark blue hand-knitted cardigan. She had a single string of pearls around her neck and wore pearl earrings. There were a few streaks of grey in her hair. It was almost impossible to believe that this was the woman who, on Friday nights and Saturday lunchtimes, could be seen removing her clothes in a saloon bar. She was a good looking woman and she had a fine figure.

I know that one shouldn't entertain preconceived notions about people but I still couldn't help thinking that she just didn't look like a striptease artiste.

I suddenly wondered if she ever glued tassels to her nipples and if she could make one tassel go round clockwise while making the other go round anticlockwise.

'I've got a confession to make, doctor,' she said, when she had sat down. 'And I need your advice.'

I waited, as though I didn't know her secret.

'Gordon was put on part-time work a year or so ago,' she said. 'You know he works at the timber yard outside Barnstaple? On the road out to Bideford?'

I nodded.

'Well, things haven't been too good at the yard and all the workers were put on a three day week.'

'I had heard something about it,' I said. Several of my patients work at the timber yard.

'So we had difficulty in paying the rent and making ends meet,' said Carole. 'I look after the money, I always have done because Gordon doesn't like dealing with paperwork and the cheque book, and it's been a real worry. The electricity company threatened to cut us off a few months ago and we're still behind with the payments. I offered to get a job to help out but Gordon wouldn't hear of it. He's a bit old-fashioned in that respect. And, besides, the sort of jobs I could get wouldn't have helped much. There's nothing in the village and if I got a job cleaning in Barnstaple I wouldn't earn enough to pay the petrol and car parking charges.'

I didn't say anything; I just sat and listened and waited.

It was strange to listen to the beginning of the story when I already knew the end of it but I couldn't tell Carole that Gordon had been to see me. I think that doctor-patient confidentiality is the foundation of the relationship between doctors and patients. And so I didn't say anything.

Carole swallowed hard and plucked at her cardigan. 'I don't know how to tell you what I've been doing,' she said. 'But I need to tell someone because I don't want my marriage to be at risk.'

'Just tell me,' I said. 'I can't help you unless you tell me what you're worried about.'

'You won't judge me?'

'Of course not!'

'I've got a sister who lives in Wolverhampton,' said Carole. 'She's three years younger than me and a single mother with two kids. Her husband walked out on her a few years ago. I talked to her about my worries about money and she confessed that for several years she had been working as a stripper in a pub near where she lives. She said that they paid really well for a few hours work a week.' Carole started to blush. 'I was shocked when she told me what she'd been doing because I always thought strippers were, well, you know, what we used to call 'scrubbers'.'

There was a pause. Carole had started to cry.

I reached across the desk and silently handed her a box of paper handkerchiefs.

'I thought that she meant that she was on the game, you know, working as a prostitute, but she said she wasn't. She said it was nothing like that. All she did was go to the pub three or four evenings a week and take off her clothes. She said it was easy to learn how to do it in a sexy sort of way. You have to wear something a bit special, of course. You can't strip when you're wearing a pair of old jeans and a jumper. She told me that she got paid more for three or four evenings than she could earn working full-time in a factory or a shop. And she said the customers weren't much trouble. Occasionally, one would ask her to go home with him but she'd just politely tell him 'No thank you' and that would be the end of it. The pub owner didn't let the customers harass the girls because he didn't want to lose them and, more importantly, I suppose, because he didn't want to lose his entertainment licence. I think the police and the magistrates can be quite severe about things like that.'

'Did she suggest that you tried something similar?'

'Not directly,' said Carole. 'But when I'd spoken to her I rang Gilly and asked her if she knew of any pubs in the area which employ strippers.'

'Gilly Parsons at the Duck and Puddle?'

Carole nodded and then blew her nose. I got up, moved the waste basket so that it was next to her chair, and then sat down again. Carole put the used tissue into the basket and took a fresh one from the box. 'Yes, I thought she'd be bound to know if any pubs in North Devon had work for strippers. She told me of a pub that she knew and she gave me a name and a telephone number to ring.'

I waited.

'The owner of the pub was very nice about it,' she said. 'He said he had a couple of young girls but wanted a more mature woman because he'd heard on the grapevine that the customers in other pubs sometimes liked to see an older woman taking her clothes off. He arranged for one of his regular girls to give me a few tips, lessons I suppose, and I passed an audition. That was the most embarrassing thing, really; taking my clothes off on a wet Wednesday morning with just this fat bloke watching me. But he was very professional about it. It wasn't as sordid as it sounds. He said he'd give me a trial and that obviously went well because I've been working there ever since.'

'As a stripper?'

Carole was now bright red. She nodded. 'We get paid more than the barmaids get for working the whole week and I just work Friday evenings and Saturday lunchtimes.'

'So you do it just for the money?'

'Oh yes.'

'Everything is fine between you and Gordon?'

'Oh, absolutely! I love him very much. And I think he loves me. I know he does.'

'What did Gordon say about it?' I asked her.

I knew, of course, that she hadn't told Gordon. But I couldn't tell her that I knew that. This whole thing was getting very complicated and I was having a job remembering who knew what and what I was supposed to know.

'I didn't tell him,' said Carole. 'I told him I was going to exercise classes.' She half smiled. 'It is a sort of exercise, I suppose. Dancing about on a tiny stage and taking off your clothes without falling over or bumping into someone. I've actually lost some weight.'

I nodded. 'And that's all that's involved?'

She looked at me.

'Taking off your clothes? That's all you do?'

She blushed an even deeper red. 'Oh, I see what you mean. Oh yes, I just take off my clothes. I don't sleep with any of the customers if that's what you mean. I wouldn't anyway, not in a million years. I'm a very loyal and faithful wife, but Geoff, the fellow who owns the pub, was very plain about that. He doesn't allow any of the girls to have sex with the customers – especially not for money. He says he'd lose his licence and probably end up in prison so he's very strict about it.'

'And Gordon doesn't know anything? He doesn't know where you go?'

'Well, that's the thing,' said Carole. 'He didn't. He used to think I was going to exercise classes. I wasn't sure how he'd take it so I thought an innocent fib wouldn't do any harm. He has never liked the idea of my working and although he's no prude, I didn't know how he'd feel if he found out that I was stripping to pay the bills. To be honest we really do need the money. As I say, I look after the finances and I don't think Gordon realises just how short things have been since he went on to working part-time. I didn't think there was any chance of him finding out. He doesn't really go to pubs, except to the local ones. But he found out.'

'Ah.' I said.

I was using up a year's supply of monosyllabic responses.

'He was at the pub last Friday,' she said. 'I didn't see him at first but I know he was there and I know he saw me. Well, he could hardly not see me, could he? And he could hardly not recognise me. He's seen me naked often enough. And all I was wearing was a wig and a lot of make up.' She swallowed and started to play with the pearls around her neck. 'But what was he doing there anyway?' she asked indignantly. 'What was he doing at a strip club?'

I was, I admit, a bit surprised by the speed with which she had switched from guilt to questioning Gordon's presence in the pub where she was stripping.

But it was a fair enough question.

'Did you tell him that you'd seen him there, in the pub?'

She shook her head. 'I think we both sort of pretended it hadn't happened.'

'Very English!' I said.

She looked at me, puzzled.

'A man goes to a strip show and sees, to his surprise, that his wife is one of the strippers. He doesn't say anything when they both get home. And the wife, who saw her husband in the audience, doesn't say anything either. They both pretend they weren't there. I think that's a pretty English sort of response.'

Carole smiled. It was the first smile since she'd come into the surgery. 'I see what you mean,' she said. 'You can't imagine two Italians behaving like that, can you?'

'You two have to talk,' I told her. 'You have to tell him what you're doing. And you have to explain why. And you have to assure him that all you're doing is taking off your clothes. And you have to let him explain to you why he was there. He may have a perfectly innocent explanation.'

'How can he have an innocent explanation for going to a strip show?'

'You have a fairly innocent explanation for stripping,' I pointed out. 'You haven't exactly become a stalwart member of the sex industry. You're just doing your bit to help make ends meet.'

She thought about this for a moment. 'I suppose so,' she admitted at last. She stopped playing with her pearls and started picking at her tweed skirt.

'So you have to tell him why you've been taking off your clothes,' I repeated.

'Would you tell him?'

Crumbs, I thought, this was getting complicated.

How could I tell him something that he already knew? And I couldn't tell Carole that he already knew.

'I want you both to come and see me tomorrow evening,' I told her. 'I'll make sure I've spoken to Gordon by then. I'll tell him what you told me. But then you both have to talk this whole thing through.'

'The problem is that if I give up the stripping we won't be able to afford to live,' she said.

'Can I ask you a personal question?'

She laughed. 'It can hardly be any more personal than the stuff we've already talked about!'

'Do you enjoy what you do? Taking off your clothes in the pub?'

'Well, I do it for the money.'

'I understand. But do you enjoy what you do? Some people like their work, some hate their work and some put up with it. How do you feel about what you now do for a living?'

There was a long pause. 'I do enjoy it,' said Carole at last. 'It's a real ego booster. Especially to a woman my age. I don't even mind when one or two of the punters try to grope me. They're easy enough to stop. But it's flattering to know that they want to.' She paused and played with her pearls again. 'I'm being painfully honest with you, doctor.'

'I know you are,' I said. 'I appreciate that. But it's important that you know how you feel about what you're doing. And it helps if I know too.'

'Tomorrow evening then?' she said, standing up.

'Tomorrow evening,' I agreed.

I was, by now, beginning to see the light. There wasn't a lot of light, it is true, but there was enough for me to see that there might a solution to this seemingly intractable problem involving the ecdysiast and her husband.

When Gordon next appeared in the surgery I told him that I wanted him to come to the evening surgery later that day. 'Bring Carole with you,' I told him. 'And we'll talk this through together.'

I could not, of course, tell him that I had already spoken to Carole and nor could I tell him that she had seen him watching her in the pub where she worked.

After Gordon had left, I dealt with a pile of paperwork which Miss Johnson had placed on my desk when she brought me my post-surgery cup of tea.

I then went out on my visits.

It was, to be honest, a relief to be out and about in the village, and to deal with straightforward medical problems.

It was autumn, and it was an autumn I can remember vividly.

Frank Parsons, who has a unique way with words and who was, in his heavy drinking days, known to make the occasional faux pas, once famously said that autumn was one of his four favourite seasons. It's certainly in my top four.

The autumn we had that year was so spectacular that I suspect that even Frank, who is not easily impressed, would have put it into his top three seasons.

We were enjoying the sort of rare collation of colours which Americans enjoy every year; particularly those Americans who live in New England; in Vermont, Massachusetts, Maine, Connecticut, Rhode Island and New Hampshire.

The spectacular colours which are a feature of autumn (or fall) in those parts of the United States are a result of very unusual circumstances. There is usually an early cold spell at the very end of the summer, followed by an extended period of sunshine in October. As autumn develops, the sap is prevented from entering the leaves by the growth of new, hard cells at the base of each twig. The result is that the leaves start to die and the green colour fades.

The glorious reds, yellows and oranges which make autumn so spectacular, only appear when there is the right mixture of cold, warmth and sunshine. In areas where the weather is too cold, too soon, the leaves fall quickly and never have a chance to develop those stunning colours, let alone to show them. In parts of the country where the weather is too warm, the leaves are already breaking up and falling from the trees by the time the sap has risen.

In Devon, and in England in general, there is usually too much rain for those marvellous autumn colours to develop properly. The soil in our part of the world, is too rich and moist and as a result the leaves stay green until the moment they are killed by early winter frosts. Moreover, the colours of an English autumn are not usually properly visible because the skies are too grey and gloomy and oppressive; the trees are likely to be hidden behind curtains of mist and rain.

The sort of autumn which the locals take for granted in New England occurs so rarely in Old England that when it does happen it inspires motorists to stop their cars, pull onto the verge and just sit and stare at an orchestral symphony for the eyes; a symphony conducted by nature, displaying every red, orange, yellow and brown imaginable.

And that's what happened that day.

Everywhere I looked there were trees which looked as though they had been painted with the aid of Turner's palette: silver birch, alder, hornbeam, beech, poplar, sweet chestnut, ash, hazel, huge English oaks, slightly smaller sessile oaks, wych elms and red oaks with their brilliant orange-red leaves. Everywhere I looked there was colour. Woodlands and copses and spinneys were ablaze. For once the fruits of autumn, conkers, acorns, beechnuts and hazelnuts took second place to the leaves of the trees.

Fifteen minutes after I left the surgery I was standing beside the car, parked no more than half a mile from the surgery, admiring the scenery.

The weather was unseasonably warm and it was the most spectacular autumn I had ever seen. As I stood there, enjoying the rare sight of an autumn in full glory, I went over what Carole and Gordon had told me and I felt my mind clearing. It seemed to me that the Singers' problem wouldn't take too much sorting out.

There were five visits to do that day.

Three of them were routine visits to elderly patients whom I liked to check on once every week or two.

It only took me a few minutes to call in and check that all was well and while I was there I always delivered whatever routine prescriptions might be necessary. Actually, I usually delivered whatever pills or creams might be needed, rather than taking prescriptions. It was far easier for me to do this than to expect the patients to find someone to call at the surgery on their behalf to turn their prescriptions into medication.

The other two calls I made were also fairly straightforward. Compared to the Singers they were very straightforward calls.

The first of these visits was to a couple called Sam and Evelyn Polger.

People who know their names but have never met them assume that he is called Sam and she is called Evelyn. But they're wrong if they do make this assumption because Mrs Polger is called Sam and Mr Polger was Christened Evelyn. (This is not as confusing as it could be. The author Evelyn Waugh was at one time married to a woman who was also called Evelyn. That must have led to some real confusion – especially with the morning mail.)

Whenever I see the Polgers, I am reminded how often I make erroneous judgements based on the names of people we meet. We all have preconceived notions about names and these notions are fed by our previous experiences. If, when we were at school, we knew a Cuthbert who was a bit wet we will assume that anyone called Cuthbert must be a bit wet. If we knew a Nigel who was the Captain of Sport, and a great hero, then we will tend to have respect for people called Nigel.

Sometimes, of course, our prejudices are fed by characters we've met only in books and films.

So, for example, the only Bertie I've ever known is Bertie Wooster, the character in P.G.Wodehouse's books about Jeeves. And so I tend to assume that anyone called Bertie must be a bit like Bertie Wooster.

The only Guy I've heard of was Guy Gibson, the World War II dambusters hero, and so to me anyone called Guy must be a heroic sort of fellow.

To others these names will, of course, probably mean something entirely different.

Anyway, Mr Polger is called Evelyn and Mrs Polger is called Sam and they have three dogs called Pickles, Chutney and Relish.

Mrs Polger is a naturalist who writes books about the countryside. She wrote one called *Squirrels in the Attic* and another called *Pheasants on the Lawn*.

Mr Polger, who did something incomprehensible at a bank in the City, presses flowers and creates pictures which he frames. He also plays the euphonium and has an extraordinary collection of Victorian pocket knives. They're a lovely couple, both in their late sixties. The two of them are terrified of hospitals.

It was Mr Polger who had asked me to visit.

After apologising for not being able to come to the surgery at Bilbury Grange, he told me that he hadn't been able to pass urine for more than 24 hours and that he felt that there might be something wrong with his bladder.

'It isn't your bladder,' I told him, when I had examined him. His bladder was massively enlarged and easy to feel. 'It's your prostate gland. It's enlarged and it has compressed your urethra – with the result that the urine can't get out of your bladder.'

'Is there anything you can do?' asked Mr Polger. 'It's a terribly uncomfortable feeling.'

I told him that he needed to be catheterised, a simple process which involves pushing a thin tube up the urethra into the bladder so that the bladder can be emptied. It's a quick and easy solution but, unfortunately, only a temporary one.

'I'd prefer to send you into hospital to have this done,' I told him. 'But I know you absolutely hate those places and if you really don't want to go into hospital I can do it for you here. I've got a catheter in the boot of the car.'

'Oh, do it here, please, doctor,' said Mr Polger.

I told him that I would do the catheterisation myself but warned him that he might, in due course, have to go the hospital to have his prostate gland checked.

'Is it cancer?' asked Mrs Polger, clearly trying to be brave.

I told her that I had absolutely no reason to suspect that her husband had cancer. 'I think his prostate is just enlarged,' I said. 'It happens often in men over the age of 60.'

'Does it mean I need to have an operation?' asked Mr Polger, who was clearly terrified of the prospect of surgery.

'Maybe,' I admitted. 'But maybe we can get away without troubling the surgeons.'

I told him that I had read reports showing that it was sometimes possible to reduce an enlarged prostate gland by taking the herb saw palmetto. I told him that he could obtain a supply from a local health food store and that I'd seen evidence that it could reduce the size of an enlarged prostate and help reduce the symptoms caused by a prostate gland which had grown too big. I also suggested that he might benefit from eating sunflower seeds which are a good source of zinc – another substance which is essential for a healthy prostate gland.

It took only a few minutes to fetch the catheter from the car and to perform the simple procedure.

When I left the Polgers half an hour later, they were both much relieved and much less fearful than they had been when I'd arrived.

Practising medicine as a country doctor can sometimes be quite simple but enormously satisfying.

My second visit was to a couple called Dawn and Jack Atkins. In their case, her real name is Phyllis but everyone calls her Dawn. His name is Jack and he is called Jack. They, like the Polgers, are retired.

When she was younger, Dawn was a singer and a member of a quartet called the Dawn Chorus. I made a fool of myself when she first told me this. 'How did they manage to find four girls all called Dawn?' I asked. She raised an exquisitely manicured eyebrow, didn't say anything but just looked at me.

'Were any of you called Dawn?' I asked as the truth dawned on me.

'We had an Elspeth, a Lettice, a Joan and me, a Phyllis,' she replied. 'We didn't actually have a Dawn. But we had a manager whose mother was called Dawn. He thought up the name and we thought it was clever so we became the Dawn Chorus.'

'We nearly had a recording contract once,' she told me. 'But things went wrong, I never did find out what the problem was, but instead of signing us, the recording company signed some fellow with a ukulele called George Formby.' She grinned. 'I bet they regretted that mistake!'

'Instead of George Formby, they could have had the Dawn Chorus?'

'They could, indeed!' She had laughed uproariously. 'Four Dawns for the price of one.'

Jack had been a sales representative for a company which made light fittings. He had travelled regularly around Europe and the Far East. He was one of those people who had a natural facility with languages and he spoke French, German, Spanish and Italian fluently and could 'get by' in Mandarin and Russian.

When I called at the Atkins's cottage I found Jack waiting for me at the front door.

'It's Dawn,' he told me, clearly agitated. 'She's got a terrible pain in her leg.'

I followed him up the stairs of their tiny but immaculate cottage. Dawn was lying on top of the bed. She was fully dressed and perfectly made up. She looked frightened and was not her usual ebullient self, though she smiled and tried to joke when she saw me.

'At last I've managed to get you into my bedroom,' she said.

'But our luck's not with us,' I said, carrying on with the joke. 'Jack's here too.'

'Foiled!' said Dawn.

And then she burst into tears.

'Damn!' she said, taking an embroidered handkerchief from her sleeve and dabbing at her eyes. 'I was going to be brave.'

I sat down on a dining chair which Jack had already placed beside the bed and took her hand. 'What's the matter?'

'I've got this absolutely terrible pain in the calf of my left leg,' she told me. 'I'm worried that it might be a deep vein thrombosis.'

'Let the doctor have a look at it before you start leaping to conclusions,' said Jack softly, from somewhere behind me.

I examined Dawn's leg. It was red and clearly tender. 'Does it hurt when you move it?'

She nodded.

'It hurts if you walk?'

'Yes, walking is painful.'

I took a tape measure and a felt tipped pen out of my black bag. I measured six inches below the bottom of her left patella and made a small mark on her leg. I then did the same thing on her right leg.

'What's that for?' asked Dawn.

'I'm going to measure both calves to see if one is bigger than the other. I want to see if there is any swelling. The pen mark helps make sure that I measure both calves at the same point.'

She nodded.

I measured her calf and found that the left calf was nearly an inch bigger than her right calf.

'I'm afraid I think your diagnosis is right,' I told her.

She probably knew this anyway, but I explained that a deep vein thrombosis is a blood clot which forms inside a vein and which may completely block the flow of blood. The danger is that the clot, or a part of it, may break free and travel up to the lungs or the heart.

I didn't tell Dawn and Jack (though I suspect that they already knew) that a deep vein thrombosis can be dangerous – even fatal.

'What's caused it?' asked Dawn.

The risk of developing a deep vein thrombosis is greater among people who have varicose veins, smoke, are overweight, have recently had surgery, have heart disease, are bedbound or are taking the contraceptive pill.

None of those things applied to Dawn.

'It can sometimes just happen, particularly in people who are over 60,' I told her.

'We've just come back from Milan,' said Jack. 'Do you think that being on the plane could have caused it? Aeroplanes seem to be very cramped these days.'

'That's because we fly in the cheap seats and when you flew for business your company always paid for the expensive seats,' said Dawn.

'The expensive seats are three or four times the price,' said Jack apologetically.

'I know, dear,' said Dawn. 'I was just explaining why the aeroplane seemed so cramped.'

'Being stuck on the plane could have caused it,' I agreed. 'Next time you fly, make sure that you wriggle your feet and massage your lower legs and feet regularly. And clench your calf muscles every quarter of an hour or so to stimulate your blood circulation.'

'I don't think we'll be flying again,' said Dawn. 'Will we Jack?'

'I'm happy to stay at home from now on,' said Jack firmly. 'Airports are so busy these days that flying has become a bit of a nightmare.'

'So, what can you do about it, doctor?' asked Dawn.

'I'm afraid I'm going to have to send you into the hospital in Barnstaple,' I told her. 'You need to have treatment to dissolve the clot. And you really need to be in hospital so that the doctors can give you exactly the right amount of the drug needed to dissolve the clot.'

'I thought as much,' said Dawn quietly.

'I've got your case packed,' said Jack. 'Two clean nighties, dressing gown, slippers, soap bag, a purse with some money in it, those two new magazines you bought but haven't read yet, a paperback from your 'Not yet read' shelf, and a box of paper tissues.'

'Don't forget to put in my make-up bag,' said Dawn. 'But wait until the doctor's gone and I've tidied myself up.'

'How long will she need to be in hospital?' asked Jack.

'Just a few days,' I told him.

I turned to Dawn. 'But you'll have to take medication for a while after you get home.'

I then borrowed their telephone and rang the ambulance service to request an ambulance. When I'd done that I rang the hospital, spoke to the house physician on duty and arranged for Mrs Atkins to be admitted.

Theoretically, I should have telephoned the hospital first to make sure that there was a bed available. But Bilbury is a good distance from the ambulance station in Barnstaple and I wanted to have the ambulance on its way without any delay.

I spent what was left of the afternoon writing the first part of an article I had promised to produce for a magazine I worked for occasionally. Mrs Singer was making ends meet by taking off her clothes in a pub in Barnstaple. I was making ends meet by writing books and articles. When you stop and think about it there isn't all that much difference. We all do what we can to keep a roof over our heads and food in our larders.

And then it was time for the evening surgery.

I had asked Gordon to come along fairly late on so that I could see him and his wife at the end of the evening surgery. I had a feeling that we might take some time to talk through the couple's problem and I didn't want to have a lot of patients sitting in the waiting room wondering what was taking so long.

Once they had both sat down, I asked Gordon to begin by explaining to Carole how he came to be in the pub on the evening when his wife was performing.

When he'd done that, I asked Carole to explain how she came to be taking off her clothes in public.

'You should have said,' said Gordon after a while.

'I know,' said Carole. 'I'm sorry I didn't say anything.'

71

'I wouldn't have minded.'

'They pay very well,' said Carole. 'And I'm only taking my clothes off.'

'You looked wonderful,' said Gordon. 'You're very good at it.'

'Do you think so?'

'I was very proud of you.'

'You weren't ashamed?'

'Why on earth should I be ashamed?'

'Because I was taking my clothes off in front of all those men.'

'So what? They cheered you. They loved you.'

'Would you like me to stop?'

'We need the money don't we?'

'We'd be in a bit of trouble without it.'

'Do you enjoy it?'

There was a silence.

'Yes, I do,' said Carole, softly. 'It makes me feel young again.'

'Would you like to carry on?'

'Do you want me to?'

'Would you like me to drive you there and back?'

'You'd come with me?'

'I could be your chauffeur and a sort of road manager.'

'That would be nice.'

'And if you want we could perhaps even take on another night if there's another pub in North Devon needing a stripper.'

'Well, I was asked to do Tuesdays at the Mott and Bailey, that pub in South Molton, but I turned them down because I didn't think you'd believe that I was taking three exercise classes. I could ring them up and see if they still need someone.'

'Well, Tuesdays would be fine. And South Molton is no further than Barnstaple.'

At this point I decided that my presence was no longer necessary and so I coughed lightly.

They both thanked me and left holding hands.

Apart from starting things off I don't think I had said a word during the entire consultation.

There had been times during the previous 24 hours when I'd been convinced that things were going to end up badly.

But in truth, it isn't often that things end up so happily.

When the surgery was over I poured myself an extra-large malt whisky as a small celebration. It felt as though it had been a long day.

I then telephoned the Polgers to see how Mr Polger was getting on. His wife told me that he was fine; he was passing urine again normally and he felt much more comfortable than he'd been that morning.

I'd hardly put the telephone down before it rang again.

It was the duty doctor from the hospital in Barnstaple.

My heart jumped when I knew who was calling. I only had one patient in the hospital and hospital doctors don't ring GPs to give them hourly updates on what their patients are eating.

The doctor was ringing to tell me that Dawn Atkins had died a few minutes earlier.

They had put up a drip and she had been receiving anti-clotting medication for several hours. Everything should have been fine but the clot, or a piece of it, must have broken off, travelled upwards and lodged in her heart.

She'd had a massive heart attack and despite all their efforts she had died.

'Does Mr Atkins know?' I asked.

'That's why I'm ringing you,' said the doctor. 'He went home about an hour ago. Everything seemed fine and we told him to come back in tomorrow. We were hoping you could tell him.'

I put the telephone down and could feel tears in my eyes.

In a small village, where the doctor knows all his patients and regards them as friends, the death of a patient is a very painful business.

I went into the kitchen to tell Patsy that I had to go out. She was making dinner.

'Can you hold our meal for an hour?'

'What's wrong?' She knew from my face that this was no routine call.

I told her. We hugged for a few moments. I then went out to the car and drove to the Atkins's cottage.

There are some aspects of being a country doctor which I hate very much indeed.

The Case of the Wobbly Film Star

The whole thing had started eight or nine weeks earlier.

Patsy and I had just finished dinner and we had sat down to listen to the fifth in a series of long playing records of choral work by Thomas Tallis. Patchy and Adrienne Fogg had given us a set of records by the composer for our anniversary. Until we had received the gift, neither Patsy nor I had ever heard of him but Patchy is something of an expert on old English music. Thomas Tallis was a 16th century composer who produced an enormous number of pieces of music in his 80 years. Patsy and I had decided that Tallis's music is divine in both senses of the word.

And then the telephone rang.

The caller was Mrs Whiffle who was ringing to say that her mother had tripped and fallen. She apologised, admitted that she didn't think her mother had broken any bones, but said she would be grateful if I would pop along and give her mother a quick check up – just to make sure that everything was all right.

Dr Brownlow, my predecessor and erstwhile employer, once told me that nothing good ever happens at 4 a.m. He was right about that, of course. (Dr Brownlow was a wise old owl who was rarely wrong about anything). But, I would go a little further for in my experience as a country doctor nothing good happens between the hours of 7 p.m. and 7 a.m. If the telephone at Bilbury Grange rings during those twelve hours, then the problem is usually significant. It may not be critical or even threatening, but it will be significant to the patient or to the relative or friend who has made the call. My patients tend to be thoughtful; they don't bother me out of hours unless they think the problem is a serious one. They aren't always right, of course. Sometimes the problem is relatively trivial and can be easily conquered with the aid of an injection, a tablet or a few words of quiet explanation and a good sized healthy dollop of country comfort.

I learned early on in my career in general practice that at no time does the reassurance of a doctor count for more than in the dark, small hours of the night, for it is in the darkness of the night when reality is of least significance.

I have noticed, indeed, that when a call is made at 9 p.m. in the dead of winter, the caller is almost certain to be more agitated than when a call is made at 9 p.m. in the summer. The very fact that the world is dark can be enough to accentuate, even exaggerate, our quite natural fears.

When we are nervous and frightened, and possibly alone with our apprehensions, suspicions and imaginations, what matters is not what is really wrong but what we think is wrong and what we think is likely to happen next. As with ghouls and evil spirits, ghosts and banshees, we are alarmed by the unknown and we worry, inevitably, about what may be happening and what might happen next.

Patsy turned off the record player (I asked her to carry on listening but she said she didn't want to listen by herself and would do some housework until I returned) and I put on my coat and picked up my black bag.

Olga and Algernon Whiffle have only been in the village a couple of years but they have already established themselves as well-liked inhabitants; they both have time for the elderly in the village and they always express an interest (without being nosy or gossipy) in the history of the village and its inhabitants.

In rural areas it is often said that it can take decades, if not generations, for newcomers to feel part of a village community and that is often true. I suspect that it is particularly in parts of Devon and Cornwall where communities often feel isolated and cut off from the world and where the geography, the geology, the weather and the absence of main roads or railway lines mean that the isolation is often very real rather than merely conceptual.

However, if the newcomers make a genuine and polite interest in the community where they have chosen to make their home, and they are prepared to put themselves out a little and to learn a little about their neighbours and the environment in which they have chosen to place themselves, then the process can be speeded up dramatically.

Mr and Mrs Whiffle were good examples of how it is perfectly possible to move into a community and then, within a relatively short space of time, succeed in becoming part of it.

The Whiffles have a curious history which is not unique but is rare enough to be unusual.

Before they moved to Bilbury, they lived in a village just outside Bristol and they were neighbours.

Mr Whiffle, and the woman who was then his wife, lived in a smart, modern detached house on a small estate of a dozen newly built homes. The woman who is now Mrs Whiffle was then called Mrs Hambledon and she lived in the house next door with Mr Hambledon, the man to whom she was then married.

Mrs Whiffle (the former Mrs Whiffle) worked in Bristol where she had a good job as an artist in an advertising agency. Mr Hambledon, who also worked in Bristol, was an architect. Since both the woman who was then Mrs Whiffle and Mr Hambledon worked in the centre of Bristol, no more than a quarter of mile away from each other, it was agreed that they would travel into work together. This would enable them to make a considerable saving on petrol, car parking charges and so on. Mr Whiffle and Mrs Hambledon agreed that it was a sensible idea.

Mr Whiffle worked as a journalist on a small newspaper in Taunton and the woman who was then Mrs Hambledon didn't have an outside job but kept herself fully occupied with a variety of responsibilities and obligations in the village. She was secretary of the local Drama Society, chairwoman of the Wives Group at the church and an active member of a national charity which delivered meals to lonely, elderly folk who lived in the area.

And then both families were hit by a thunderbolt.

Mrs Whiffle and Mr Hambledon announced that they had fallen in love with each other, that they had indeed been having an affair for some time, and that it was their intention to move into Bristol and live in a spacious new apartment which they had agreed to purchase together. There were, inevitably, many tears, the inevitable accusations of betrayal, and, in due course, some rather acrimonious negotiations and two divorces.

In due course, Mr Whiffle and Mrs Hambledon, finding themselves alone and thrown together as solitary neighbours, began to socialise a little.

Neither of them had children at home and so there were no impediments to what began as a purely social relationship; a practical and convenient way of dealing with their inevitable loneliness.

They went to the cinema together. They went shopping in Bristol together. At the weekends they ate out at village pubs. They discovered that they shared a good many interests and enthusiasms. And, thrown together by these stressful and unusual circumstances, the friendship turned into something more. They cried together, they laughed together, they held hands and just under a year after their partners had left, the two became lovers.

After that, they decided that it would make perfect sense to live together and to marry. After all, there were no legal or moral constraints to prevent their doing so.

As the former Mrs Whiffle had become the present Mrs Hambledon, so the former Mrs Hambledon became the present Mrs Whiffle. It all sounds strange but I suspect that this variety of wife and husband swapping is much commoner than is generally believed. It is something I had come across once or twice before.

Once they had agreed to marry, the new Whiffles realised that there were practical problems to be overcome.

Both of the Whiffles had large mortgages which they found difficult to meet.

But which house should they keep and which one should they sell?

After some discussions they decided to make a clean break; to sell both houses and to move away from the area.

They decided that they would retire and move to Devon, a county for which they had both always had an affection. They did their sums and decided that they could make a go of things.

And Mrs Whiffle (the new Mrs Whiffle) asked her new husband if it would be too much of a burden if her mother, who was a widow and in her early eighties, came to live with them.

Mrs Whiffle's mother was a retired actress and, like all actresses who have appeared in at least one film, she liked to describe herself as a former film star. This seemed to me to be an entirely understandable, eminently reasonable and utterly harmless conceit.

Mrs Whiffle's mother had appeared in several films made in the 1930s, when she had rather specialised in playing gay young widows and divorcees, but in her later years she had, I believe, been better known for her work in the London theatre. Her real name (which had for years taken second place to her stage name and the use of which even now was confined to communications with the Inland Revenue, the Passport Office and all parts of the National Health Service) was Mathilda Ruthvens.

She once told me, with the sort of pride people always exhibit when they have a name with a deal of history attached to it, that Ruthvens was the family name of the Earls of Gowrie who, in the year 1600, kidnapped James VI of Scotland, who was later to become James I of England. She said that the Scots were so annoyed by this insult that they had passed a name banning the use of the name of Ruthvens for evermore. However, like all silly laws which are passed in perpetuity, the law was eventually forgotten and ignored. Her husband, the source of the name, had died in 1956 and Mrs Ruthvens had lived alone ever since.

Mrs Ruthvens had a cottage in Sussex which she agreed to sell and she said that was very happy to put the proceeds towards the purchase of a suitable home with her daughter and new son-in-law.

Mr Whiffle said he wouldn't mind at all having his mother-in-law sharing their home. As he said, the world can be a dreary, dull place; it needs more former film stars wandering about the place and, in his words: 'If you are offered a chance of sharing your home with a film star you'd have to be mad to turn it down'.

This apparent superficiality hid a genuine affection.

When I arrived at the Whiffle's house, Mrs Ruthvens was lying on a sofa, though since it had a backrest at only one end I expect she would have preferred to think of it as a chaise longue, and she was looking distinctly irritable about being treated like an invalid. She was, as usual, wearing enough make-up to satisfy the requirements of the audience in the seats at the back of the Dress Circle at one of the large London theatres. Her false eyelashes were the biggest I'd ever seen. She wore a splendid wig to disguise the fact that her hair, having been permed and curled and brutalised for decades, was now thinning and no longer the crowning glory it had doubtless once been.

'I just fell, doctor,' she said, rather crossly. 'There was no need to call you out. There's nothing whatsoever wrong with me. My daughter fusses too much. I'm just another old lady getting a bit unsteady on her feet.' She winked at me; a gesture for which she had once been rather famous. 'I probably had too many glasses of sherry before dinner.'

'She had no sherry before dinner,' said Mrs Whiffle, who seemed both apologetic and worried. 'And she had no wine with dinner. And no brandy after it.'

I carefully examined Mrs Ruthvens but happily found no sign of any injury. I took her blood pressure. The systolic was raised a little, but nothing worrying. I listened to her heart. Everything was ticking along nicely; better, indeed, than might be expected in a piece of equipment which had been functioning perfectly for the best part of a century. I looked into her ears, checked her eyesight and performed other simple tests which might have offered a hint of any underlying abnormality.

I found absolutely nothing wrong.

'Do you ever suffer from dizziness?' I asked her.

'Never!'

'Have there been any changes in your eating or drinking habits?' She shook her head.

'Have you found anything wrong?' asked Mrs Whiffle.

'You're as fit as a fiddle!' I told Mrs Ruthvens.

'That's good to know.'

(I know that nothing annoys an elderly patient more completely than the doctor providing information to relatives, as though the patient were a motor car or a piece of antique furniture and the doctor an assessor offering an opinion to an owner or a would-be purchaser. And yet it is surprising just how many doctors do this.)

'Have you fallen before?' I asked Mrs Ruthvens.

'Good heavens no,' replied the actress. She stopped and thought for a moment. 'I fell off a horse in around 1937,' she said. 'I was making a film called *Robin Hood* with Errol Flynn and Olivia de Havilland and the horse they gave me was rather lively for my liking.' She stopped and allowed a small smile to appear. 'He was a devil!' she said and then, allowing three beats for the timing, added: 'Errol not the horse.' She smiled as though there was a good deal that she could tell me if she were the sort of person inclined to share such secrets.

'Would you like a cup of tea, doctor?' asked Mrs Whiffle, unexpectedly and rather loudly. 'I'm so sorry, I should have offered you something before.'

'Oh, I could tell you a few stories about Errol!' said Mrs Ruthvens, ignoring her daughter. 'Everything you've heard about him was absolutely true!'

'Or maybe a whisky?' said Mrs Whiffle, who clearly didn't want her mother telling me the secrets of her adventures with Mr Flynn. 'Doctors always drink whisky, don't they?'

'That's very kind of you,' I said. 'But no, thank you.'

'Yes, she has fallen several times quite recently,' said Mrs Whiffle, before her mother could continue with her reminiscences. I decided that she had perhaps already heard her mother's Errol Flynn stories and thought them not suitable for the occasion. 'She'll tell you that she hasn't but she has. She's fallen a number of times in the last month and almost daily in the last week or so. On Wednesday, she fell in the garden and badly grazed her arm. I nearly called you then because I thought she might have broken her forearm.'

'I tripped on a daisy,' said Mrs Ruthvens, addressing me. 'It's just my age, dear,' she said, directing the comment at her daughter. She reached out and took her daughter's hand. 'It's sweet of you to worry about me but I do wish you wouldn't fuss so.' She suddenly turned and looked at me as though she had never seen me before. 'You must think I'm absolutely ancient,' she said.

'Not at all,' I said, smiling at her. In truth she looked very good for her age. She was, I knew, 87-years-old. She looked at least fifteen years younger and the compliment was well deserved.

Age is a funny thing. It is always relative. At the age of six we think that anyone who is 14 is absolutely ancient. At 14 we consider anyone who is 20 to be aged and possibly bordering on infirm. At 70 we think that anyone who has died in their 70s must have died very young. And although some of those who are fortunate enough to wander into the 80s tend to glory in their longevity, others, like Mrs Ruthvens, regard themselves as merely having tiptoed gracefully into full maturity.

'Is it normal for older people to start falling over?' Mrs Whiffle asked me.

Mrs Ruthvens muttered something in what was clearly a stage whisper. It was clear that she objected to her daughter's use of the phrase 'older people'.

'No, it isn't normal,' I told Mrs Whiffle. 'There's no intrinsic reason why age itself should make us unstable and there is no more reason for someone in their 80s to fall over than there is for someone in their 30s to fall over – unless there is something wrong with them.'

'What sort of things?' asked Mr Whiffle, who had been sitting quietly until this moment. 'What types of illness cause someone to fall?'

'It's quite a long list,' I said. 'Joint pain and weakness, such as occur in osteoarthritis and rheumatoid arthritis, can result in falls. So can muscle weakness, often a result of a failure to do enough exercise, and foot problems which might make someone unstable.' I thought for a moment, mentally making a list of the other disorders which can result in falls. 'Obviously, a stroke can result in unsteadiness, so can poor vision, balance problems, disorders such as Meniere's disease, low blood pressure, which is usually a result of a patient taking too much medication for high blood pressure, side effects caused by prescription drugs and disorders such as Parkinson's disease.'

I paused again, to think.

'You've missed one,' said Mrs Ruthvens.

I looked at her and waited.

'Booze!' said Mrs Ruthvens. 'I've known a good many people who fell over after drinking too much.'

'Mother!' said Mrs Whiffle.

'It's true!' said Mrs Ruthvens. 'I should know. I've worked with Peter O'Toole, Oliver Reed and what was the name of that one who was married to Elizabeth thingy. They made that film Cleopatra together.'

'Richard Burton,' said Mrs Whiffle. 'He was married to Elizabeth Taylor.'

'Richard. Richard. Of course it was. Richard was very sweet,' said Mrs Ruthvens. 'I had a small part in Cleopatra. Did you know?'

I admitted that I hadn't known.

'I was some sort of handmaiden,' said Mrs Ruthvens. 'We were just there as decoration. Miss Taylor made me stand at the back every time I was in a scene with her. She said she thought my bosom was too luxurious and would attract attention away from her.'

'Mother!' said Mrs Whiffle.

'It's true,' said Mrs Ruthvens. 'I had a quite splendid bosom when I was younger. I used to do what were called 'cheesecake' photographs. When we made Cleopatra, the props men used to shout into my cleavage to see if an echo came back.' She laughed.

Mrs Whiffle exchanged glances with her husband.

'You're right about the alcohol, of course,' I said. 'But as far as I can see you don't have signs of anything to make you likely to fall over.'

'There is something else,' said Mrs Whiffle. 'Mother won't like me mentioning this but her memory has been getting poor recently.'

'That's nonsense!' said Mrs Ruthvens. 'Stuff and nonsense. My memory is as good as it ever was.'

'You forget names more often than you used to,' said Mrs Whiffle.

'Just because I forgot the name of that Burton woman,' protested Mrs Ruthvens. 'And Richard.'

'It isn't just that,' said Mrs Whiffle. She turned to her husband. 'She has been more forgetful recently, hasn't she?'

Mr Whiffle nodded his agreement. 'You forgot the name of the man who runs the village shop,' he said.

'It's Johnson,' said Mrs Ruthvens. 'Something Johnson. Robert Johnson?'

'It's Peter Marshall,' said her daughter gently.

'Well I can't be expected to know the names of everyone who runs a shop,' said Mrs Ruthvens, rather defensively.

I asked Mrs Ruthvens a few simple questions, just to check out her memory. She said that Sir Alec Douglas-Home was still Prime Minister. I asked her about money. She didn't seem aware that Britain had introduced decimalisation. She said that Brighton was the nearest large town.'

I didn't want to embarrass her by telling her that the Prime Minister's name was Harold Wilson or that Barnstaple, not Brighton, was the nearest town, so I just nodded.

'Maybe we need to do a few tests,' I told her. 'I'll fix up for you to see one of the consultants at the hospital.'

'Tests!' said Mrs Ruthvens, derisively. 'What good are tests going to be?' She sounded cross and this I found surprising, partly because it was unlike her to be so aggressive and partly because of the sudden change in her mood. She pushed herself up, stood for a moment as she steadied herself with a hand on the back of a nearby chair, and then walked away. She walked slowly and rather nervously, as though afraid that she might fall, and I could not help noticing that she had a strange sort of gait, unsteady and wide legged as though she were walking along the promenade deck of a liner in a storm.

An individual's gait can tell you a good deal about any underlying pathology.

For example, the patient with Parkinson's disease will often shuffle along, failing to lift their feet more than an inch or two off the ground, and a patient with tertiary syphilis and tabes dorsalis may have a more dramatic, stamping gait.

But although the strange gait which Mrs Ruthvens exhibited seemed to suggest something specific, something I had never seen but had read about, I couldn't remember what it was.

As I headed out to my car, Mr Whiffle came with me. 'She's suffering from dementia isn't she?' He spoke softly, though the front door was closed and there was no way that his mother-in-law could hear him.

'It would seem possible,' I agreed. I was more worried about her failing to remember Richard Burton's name than her inability to remember Peter Marshall's name. 'But it's not something I'd like to diagnose after one short visit. We all have good and bad days and the elderly seem particularly prone to having their ups and downs.'

'Is it that disease beginning with an A?' asked Mr Whiffle. 'I can't remember the name of it. But I read about it in a magazine.'

'Alzheimer's?' I said.

'That's the one. Do you think that's what she has?'

'I'm really not sure,' I said. 'Not until we have some tests done.'

The surprising truth was that my only previous experience with patients with Alzheimer's disease had been when I had been a medical student, working in hospitals in and around Birmingham. In Bilbury, I had seen several patients who had dementia in varying degrees, usually fairly mild and manageable, but I had never seen a patient with Alzheimer's disease.

'Could dementia make her fall?'

'No, I don't think so,' I told him. 'That may be something else.'

With younger patients I always tried to find one diagnosis to explain all the possible signs and symptoms. But with older patients it is not uncommon for there to be more than one underlying problem causing different symptoms.

I drove back home feeling very sad. I liked Mrs Ruthvens. She was undoubtedly a 'character' and it was difficult not to be charmed by her. But there was something else that none of us had mentioned. I knew the former actress well enough to have noticed that there had definitely been a change in her personality. Her mood had changed very quickly and she had become more aggressive than she had ever been before. So there were three things going on that I needed to tie together. She was falling down a good deal, her memory was fading and her personality seemed to be changing.

The problem was that I had no idea what the underlying pathology could be. Was there one disorder responsible for everything? Or were there two or even three things going on? I knew I needed help from someone who could help me solve this particular puzzle and, if possible, point the way to a single diagnosis that would explain all Mrs Ruthven's problems.

I managed to arrange for Mrs Ruthvens to see a consultant in Exeter; a physician who specialised in the care of the elderly. The plan was that he would talk to her, examine her and subject her to a few tests in order to find out what was going on.

Two weeks later he wrote to me and told me that in his view, Mrs Ruthvens was developing the type of dementia known as Alzheimer's disease.

'There is,' he wrote, 'no way of testing for this condition (though I understand that experiments are under way which will, maybe in the 1980s, enable us to visualise what is going on in the brain). More disappointingly, there is currently no treatment for this condition.'

I telephoned the consultant and after three or four attempts I managed to speak to him. I asked him if he thought it possible that the Alzheimer's disease might be making her unsteady. He said he had never come across such a thing but that, yes, he thought it possible.

And, as far as he was concerned, that seemed to be that.

His prognosis was, to say the least, rather gloomy. He told me that he thought that Mrs Ruthvens would deteriorate steadily over the coming months and that eventually she would probably need to be admitted to a home which specialised in the care of patients with dementia.

'It's a gloomy business,' he told me. 'Worrying for the patient and distressing for the relatives and friends. Once the disease has gone past a certain point, I always think that it's the relatives who suffer most. The patient often doesn't know what's happening to them but the relatives have to stand around and watch their loved one deteriorate and gradually fall apart before their eyes. A pretty terrible thing all round.'

His solitary, practical suggestion was that Mrs Ruthvens should be fitted with some sort of address tag, containing the name and telephone number of her daughter, so that, anyone who found her wandering away from home could get in touch. When he told me this, I could feel tears forming in my eyes. I knew it was a sensible idea, and something we should eventually consider, but to think of Mrs Ruthvens, so full of life, to be labelled like a parcel was just too much.

I visited Mrs Ruthvens at home and talked to her, to her daughter and to her son-in-law.

Not surprisingly, they were all very upset by the consultant's diagnosis though I wasn't sure that Mrs Ruthvens realised precisely how awful the news really was. She seemed to be deteriorating remarkably quickly and although I could find no explanation for the new symptom she was now also complaining of headaches.

I still felt that we were all missing something.

I vaguely remembered having read something in a medical journal that was relevant. But I couldn't for the life of me think what it was.

I was desperate to find the correct diagnosis. Being close doesn't count in sport and it doesn't count in medicine, either.

After wracking my brain for a week, I mentioned the problem when I was speaking to Will, the GP in the English Midlands with whom I had studied and who was still a good friend. We spoke once a week, usually on a Saturday or a Sunday, to discuss problems we had encountered during our week's work. I found these conversations enormously helpful since, as a general practitioner working alone in a fairly remote Devonshire village, I had almost no contact with other members of the profession.

Even when we couldn't help each other, we could usually help with details of a scientific paper we had read somewhere, or the contact details of a physician or surgeon who might be able to offer a useful opinion.

I told Will about Mrs Ruthvens.

'The odd thing is,' I said, 'that she has a rather peculiar way of walking. I've never seen anything quite like it before.'

I explained that she walked with her feet wide apart, as though she were walking on an unstable surface.

'She's developing dementia and has some personality changes,' I told him. 'But the gait, and the falls, don't fit in with the consultant's diagnosis of Alzheimer's disease. I know that there could be something else going on but I'd like to try to find a single diagnosis that fits all the symptoms.'

'It couldn't be Parkinson's disease? You can get some bizarre variations?'

I had already considered Parkinson's disease but at Will's suggestion I thought about it again.

Patients with Parkinson's do sometimes suffer from a form of dementia and they do have difficulty in walking. But the gait is a shuffling one; patients cannot lift their feet off the floor properly and so steps and uneven pavements are especially dangerous. And they also have difficulty in managing hand to mouth coordination and can, for example, have problems coping with cutlery.

I thought about Mrs Ruthvens.

She just didn't look as if she had Parkinson's disease.

In my experience, patients with Parkinson's tend to have a blank face, sometimes with a ghost of a smile, and dull eyes, not focussed, apparently looking into the distance.

'No,' I said. 'I'm sure she hasn't got Parkinson's.'

'Well I haven't the foggiest what it could be,' Will admitted. 'But why don't you speak to Bussage Hill?'

I couldn't for the life of me remember knowing anyone called Bussage Hill, or why I should speak to him. I said so.

'He was in our year at medical school,' said Will. 'He had a twin brother called Chalford who was also studying medicine. They both married nurses while they were still students. You must remember them! They weren't really part of our crowd because they both lived fairly well-ordered, sensible lives. The four of them shared a terraced house in Handsworth and the Hills were the only students in our year who always wore freshly ironed shirts.'

Suddenly it came back to me. 'Was Bussage a rotund little guy with bottle glass spectacles and a funny, high-pitched giggle? He drove something small and very sensible. A Hillman Imp I think it was.'

'That's Bussage! His brother looked almost identical but didn't have the giggle.'

'So why do I want to speak to Bussage Hill?'

'He's a neurologist at Oxford. After he qualified he did a PhD in cerebrospinal fluid dynamics and now he's doing research work into dementia. I only know all this because the other day I saw a research paper written by him in one of the medical journals. I'll get a photocopy made and post it off to you. It's pretty incomprehensible stuff to be honest but the paper has all his contact details.'

And so three days later I found myself talking to Bussage Hill.

We had never been friends at medical school. Students tend to form into small groups with similar interests and Bussage and his brother had, as Will remembered, lived very different lives to the rest of us.

The one thing I could remember about Bussage was that if he had been a bicycle he would have been one of those battered old bone shakers that the owners never bother to padlock because they know that no one in or out of their right mind would have bothered to steal it.

Imagine a bicycle with two soft tyres, no working lights, a rusty frame, handlebars slightly askew and a well-worn, lopsided saddle and you'll have a good idea what Bussage would have looked like if he had been a bicycle. He may have always worn clean and neatly ironed shirts but he nevertheless managed to look as if life had given him a good battering.

Fortunately, Bussage remembered me.

It helped that he had seen some of my articles and that he'd read a couple of my books.

'Normal pressure hydrocephalus,' said Bussage, when I'd finished detailing Mrs Ruthven's symptoms. He sounded excited. 'That's what she's got.'

'What the devil is normal pressure hydrocephalus?' I asked him.

'Oh, I'm not surprised you haven't heard of it,' he said, in that rather dismissive way common among men and women who have specialised in some esoteric branch of anything. 'A couple of guys called Raymond Adams and Hakim Dow wrote a paper in the *Journal of Neurological Science* back in 1965. It's still pretty cutting edge stuff.'

He then proceeded to explain the condition to me.

'You remember that the space between the brain and the skull is filled with cerebrospinal fluid – there to protect the brain in case of injury?'

'Yes,' I replied.

I have often found that in addition to being rather superior, super specialists have difficulty in differentiating between the stuff any medical student should know and the stuff that only specialists are likely to know. The result is that they can sometimes be unintentionally patronising.

'Normally, the cerebrospinal fluid is produced, circulates and is then reabsorbed,' continued Bussage. 'Occasionally, things go wrong and the fluid isn't reabsorbed as fast as it is produced. So then the liquid accumulates in the ventricles – the spaces within the brain – and the brain is put under pressure.'

'But why is it called 'normal pressure hydrocephalus?' I asked, puzzled.

This wasn't making much sense. If there was too much cerebrospinal fluid it would make sense for the pressure to be high – not normal.

'Ah, logically, you might expect that with there being too much fluid in a confined space there would be an increase in the fluid pressure,' agreed Bussage. 'But this doesn't happen with normal pressure hydrocephalus. The intracranial pressure remains normal and the fluid pressure squashes the brain.'

'So, where does the excess fluid go?' I asked, still puzzled.

'The ventricles dilate in order to accommodate the extra fluid. And since there is only so much space within the skull the expanding ventricles, full of fluid, damage the brain.'

I was beginning to understand. This was a very strange disease indeed. 'What are the symptoms?' I asked.

'It usually starts with a funny wobbly walk and then patients show signs of dementia. After a while they start to show signs of urinary incontinence. Has your patient got urinary incontinence?'

'No,' I replied. 'No, I'm pretty sure she hasn't.'

'That's good. Then if I'm right, and I'm sure I am, then she's still in the early stages.'

'It sounds rare. Is it?'

'That's the thing. Some of the guys doing research into this reckon that it probably affects thousands of people who have been mistakenly diagnosed as suffering from Alzheimer's.'

'Is there any treatment?'

'Ah, well that's a good question,' said Bussage. 'There isn't a cure available in this country. But there's a surgeon I know in the States who's been getting amazing results by putting in a little plastic tube which he calls a shunt. The shunt helps by draining away the excess fluid. His problem is finding patients to operate on. Because no one knows about the disease he doesn't get any referrals. And he needs patients who haven't been too badly affected. If the brain has been squashed for too long then the operation doesn't really help. Can your patient come and see me? I could do a few tests and if I think that's what she's got and she's game I could ask this guy in America to include her in his trial. I've got a fairly decent grant and I might be able to swing the price of a couple of air fares to send her and a relative over there.'

He sounded terribly excited and I agreed to get in touch with the family straight away and to get back to him that same day.

When I went back to see them, the Whiffles sounded just as excited as Bussage Hill had been, though I tried to downplay expectations as much as I reasonably could.

And within an hour I had arranged for Mr and Mrs Whiffle and Mrs Ruthvens to visit Bussage at the hospital just outside Oxford where he had privileges as a visiting consultant of neurology.

From that point on things happened very quickly.

Bussage Hill's examination and tests convinced him that Mrs Ruthvens was, indeed, suffering from normal pressure hydrocephalus and four days later, Mrs Ruthvens and her daughter flew to America where the American physician repeated Bussage's tests and doubtless added a few of his own.

Less than a week after that, Mrs Ruthvens had an operation to insert a shunt to drain away the excess cerebrospinal fluid which was accumulating and putting pressure on her brain.

I have to confess that I shared their excitement.

It isn't often that a country doctor, lost in the 'sticks' as town-dwellers call the countryside, becomes involved in the discovery and treatment of a new disease, let alone manages to play a very small part in a new advance in medical science.

Mr Whiffle telephoned me every day when he had heard from his wife and he kept me fully informed.

The news of Mrs Ruthvens's trip across the Atlantic had spread around the village like wildfire (it is quite an event in Bilbury if a villager goes as far as Exeter, a trip to London is regarded as an adventure and although a few villagers do travel widely, it is a fact that for most Bilburians anything which involves passports and an aeroplane is generally considered to be on a par with space travel) and Mr Whiffle confided that he had a dozen people to call whenever he had news from our erstwhile colony.

The dozen villagers who were called with the news direct then passed it on along a telephone chain which seemed to cover most of the village.

Almost every day, several villagers would ring Bilbury Grange to let me know how Mrs Ruthvens was getting on. Patsy, who usually answers our telephone, dealt with these calls and thanked each person for their kindness in keeping us informed. I myself kept my friend Will fully informed of the progress which was made.

I had been a keen student of medical history for some years (and had for some years harboured a desire to write a small tome on the subject myself) and I had long ago become aware that major developments in medicine occur at very infrequent intervals.

It was back in the first half of the 19th century that improvements in clean water supplies, and the provision of efficient sewage facilities, helped cut down the incidence of infectious diseases which were killing millions. Infectious diseases such as cholera had a devastating effect on infant mortality rates and it was the reduction in the incidence of such disorders which had such an impact on general mortality rates.

Then, in the second half of the same century, Joseph Lister and Louis Pasteur explained the principles of antisepsis and helped show how mortality rates in the operating theatre could be cut dramatically. Ignaz Semmelweiss showed how puerperal fever could be avoided, and his work helped make pregnancy less of a life or death lottery. William Thomas Morton and John Snow developed the first anaesthetics and Rontgen introduced X-rays. Florence Nightingale revolutionised nursing and the medical profession began, at last, to impose scientific methods upon the use of age old drugs such as aspirin, morphine and digitalis.

I was conscious that, in comparison to the century which had preceded it, the 20th century had proved disappointing.

Alexander Fleming had been alert enough to spot the importance of penicillin, and the introduction of steroids and oral contraceptives had changed the world in a number of ways.

But the big steps forward in the development of medicine as a science had undeniably been taken in the 19th century. And it seemed that all we could hope for now were incremental steps; the identification of diseases which had hitherto been unknown and the discovery of new therapies.

It seemed to me that Bussage Hill and his colleagues had, doubtless through the usual mixture of hard work and good fortune, made as vital a breakthrough as had been made in my lifetime.

And when, two weeks later, Mrs Ruthvens returned home to Bilbury, I felt proud to have seen, almost at first hand, a medical development which seemed to me akin to a miracle.

Mrs Ruthvens now walked easily and confidently. Her gait was, I suspected, every bit as distinguished and as ladylike as it had been when she'd been in her theatrical prime. And the symptoms of early dementia had disappeared completely. And so, she reported with delight, had the headaches. She was, to resort to a cliché, back to her old self.

It is, I think, a fact that when you have read a book that has touched you, and has meant something to you, then that book will be with you always; never forgotten and always influencing your life in sometimes small but memorable ways.

Similarly, when you meet a character who touches your heart or soul in some way then he or she will live forever inside you.

Mrs Ruthvens had charmed me before her illness. But that, I suspect, had, although doubtless genuine, been a superficial sort of theatrical charm. Now, however, I felt blessed to know her and to have seen her resurrected from a fate which many regard as worse than death itself: the wasting of the mind while the body still thrives.

There are many within the medical profession who rather look down their noses at family doctors in general and at country doctors in particular.

We are, they say with their often condescending manner, stuck in our old ways, dealing with coughs and colds and aches and pains and relying on hospital specialists to deal with anything more than a little out of the ordinary.

But, for an hour or so at least, I felt as if I too were at the cutting edge of medical progress.

It was not, of course, a feeling which lasted for long.

An hour after I had welcomed Mrs Ruthvens back home, I had an evening surgery to conduct.

My first patient of the surgery had scabies. My second had indigestion. And my third had ears full of hardening wax which needed softening and syringing out with the aid of nothing more sophisticated than a jug full of warm water.

But I like to think they all needed me just as much as Mrs Ruthvens had done.

Two Long Screws and a Saggy Mattress

I don't think people would be queuing up to protest if I said that I was not exceptionally skilled at doing odd jobs around the house. Nor would there be any disagreement if it were alleged that I tend to make a good deal of noise and fuss when performing simple do-it-yourself tasks.

All I can say in my own defence is that in my experience, thumbs and fingers are exceptionally sensitive and respond poorly when battered by hammers, screwdrivers or other implements. It is a known anatomical fact that all ten digits are well supplied with nerves, and it seems to me to be perfectly natural to say 'Ouch' (or more) when one or other of these sensitive parts is hit with a hammer.

Indeed, I think it's probably fair to say that when there is a small job to be done at Bilbury Grange (a task around the house which is too small for me to feel comfortable about calling in a professional) there is much holding of breath and covering of ears among those who may be within a quarter of a mile or so.

The cats disappear en masse and huddle together on the bed or in the airing cupboard, the sheep run to a far corner of their field, our pig (donated to our small menagerie by kindly American visitors who won him in a skittle competition but realised they could hardly put him on an aeroplane and take him home with them) retreats into a corner of his sty and goes to sleep, and even Ben, my old and faithful Welsh sheepdog keeps his distance. Miss Johnson shuts herself in the room where she keeps the patients' files or, if she thinks things are likely to get really bad, she climbs onto her elderly sit-up-and-beg bicycle and pedals home to her cottage until she thinks the danger period is over. If we had neighbours, they would doubtless close their doors and windows and hide under the stairs. Patsy alerts the plumber (in case I puncture a pipe), the electrician (in case I put a nail through a wire), a plasterer (to repair holes in the walls), a painter and decorator (to tidy up) and the emergency services lest I set fire to the house or remove a limb in error.

Of course, if the job is a big one then I have absolutely no qualms about calling in a professional.

If there has been a gale and we have lost a few slates from the roof then I call for Mr Yates, the roofer, a fine fellow who is half man and half monkey and who finds it so easy to climb up onto our main house roof that he rarely bothers with a ladder. He jumps up onto the water butt just outside the boiler room, uses a window sill as a launching pad to climb up onto the boiler room roof, tiptoes along a valley and, within considerably less time than it would take me to find a suitable ladder, let alone put it into place, he is leaning up against one of our rather grand chimneys surveying his private world.

If the boiler stops working (it works perfectly well throughout the summer when its reliability is of little consequence but always breaks down several times during the winter months partly, I suspect, just to show that it can and partly because it enjoys the attention), then I call on Mr Bucklebury who knows precisely where to give it a thump and which of his fine collection of wrenches to use for the operation.

I have tried thumping the boiler with a wrench but this never works for me. I have watched Mr Bucklebury carefully and have concluded that this is either because I was using the wrong sort of wrench or because I didn't know the precise part of the boiler to hit.

But I always feel rather shy about calling in an expert when it is clear that the job which needs to be done would not be much of a challenge for the average ham-fisted ten-year-old child.

Tradesmen often have advertisements and visiting cards which promise 'No job too small' but that, to be blunt, is a plain old-fashioned lie. Most of the local tradesmen who live in or around Bilbury and are patients of mine but even they will sometimes baulk if asked to come out to oil a barn door or unstick a sticking letterbox.

And, to be honest, there is always the embarrassment of calling someone to deal with a trivial problem that I know, and they know, could have been dealt with by anyone who possessed a hammer, a screwdriver and a decent complement of fingers and thumbs. I feel mortified when I have to call someone out to deal with something so trivial that any reasonably capable granny could sort it out without hesitation.

It is true that I could, of course, always phone Thumper or Patchy or any one of a dozen other friends in the village. But that seems too much like taking advantage of our friendships. They would come round and sort out whatever needed sorting out. And there would be no murmur of protest or complaint or criticism. But I'd feel guilty.

The trouble is that Bilbury Grange is an old house and, like all old houses, it is prone to developing problems. There is always something that needs doing.

I used to allow small jobs to accumulate so that when I needed to call someone in I could give them a list of problems to sort out. But the trouble with that policy is that you end up having to live with something which really needs to be dealt with sooner rather than later.

A dripping tap may seem trivial, and you may think you can wait until another tap starts to drip or a radiator starts to leak or a drain gets clogged. But a tap which drips for months on end can become surprisingly annoying and instead of simply being ignored as it drips away, the constant sound of water falling onto porcelain may become a domestic form of Chinese water torture.

A door which sticks because it has warped, and which needs a little work with a file or a plane rather than a squirt of oil, can become intensely irritating.

'I'll just wait until a window gets jammed or we need a new shelf putting up and then I'll call the carpenter,' I think to myself. And for a while this seems a sensible course of action. We get used to pulling the door to and fro or we leave it open all the time.

But then something happens and the irritation returns.

We realise that there is a draft because the door is open all the time. Or someone carrying a tray of food tries to kick the door open, fails, falls and spreads crockery and sandwiches all over a large area of carpet.

It is then that we realise that the door needs dealing with now and not in three, six or twelve months' time when we have acquired a list of small jobs which will make a visit from the carpenter worthwhile.

And so, nervously and reluctantly, I have tried to learn how to deal with a few of the simplest odd jobs myself.

I have long been the proud possessor of a bow saw and an axe (for removing small branches from trees in the garden and chopping up bits of fallen timber) but there aren't many household jobs which can be tackled with a bow saw or an axe so I recently expanded my repertoire by visiting Peter Marshall's emporium and buying a few additional tools: a hammer, a set of screwdrivers (the little ones for screwing in small screws and the big ones for taking the lids off pots of paint), a pair of pliers (which I find useful for pulling out nails when they haven't gone in quite as straight as might be preferred), a file, a chisel and half a dozen spanners which, Peter Marshall assured me, would come in very handy if I ever wanted a spanner.

He wanted to sell me a spirit level and a metal tape measure but I rejected these on the grounds that I would be happy to deal with a problem and that I didn't much care about fine tuning.

He did, however, also sell me a rather fine metal tool box which, he assured me, is an essential piece of equipment for every handyman.

The box, which has space for enough equipment to build a full scale model of the Eiffel Tower, weighs around three tons when quite empty but it does look very professional.

Peter assured me that bright orange tool boxes are very fashionable though knowing him I had, and still have, a grave suspicion that the bright orange tool boxes were obtained cheaply from a wholesaler who couldn't find enough colour blind customers.

When I dig out my orange tool kit to tackle a job around the house, Patsy and I have a well-established routine. We both know that any task, however small, requires two of us.

I retrieve the tool box from wherever it is hiding and check that the hammer, the saw or the screwdriver are all in situ (these items have, I have discovered, a strange habit of escaping from captivity and hiding themselves somewhere around the house or the garden). And I also find a pair of tough gardening gloves to help protect my fingers and thumbs. The gloves don't provide a great deal of protection but they do help stop the blood from spreading everywhere.

Patsy's role is to collect together a large bottle of antiseptic, a box of fabric sticking plasters, a packet of gauze and an assortment of crepe bandages. And, as I have already suggested, to make the precautionary telephone calls: putting various experts on stand-by.

I had found the tool box, checked the contents and was psyching myself up to tackle the latest small problem (a loose doorknob) when my concentration was disturbed by the ringing of the telephone.

'Saved by the bell!' said Patsy, who sounded genuinely relieved at the interruption. 'I'll see who it is.'

She darted off, leaving me to stare at my task for the day: a wobbly doorknob.

Of course, as I knew well, no workmen worth his salt would use the word 'doorknob' these days. He would, instead, doubtless prefer to use the phrase: 'Portal Control Mechanism and Ingress/Egress Mobility Enhancement Device'.

And he would not say it was wobbly, he would say it 'required securing and restabilising'.

The object of my attention was an old-fashioned brass knob that looked as if it had probably been originally screwed into position by the skilled workmen who had first built Bilbury Grange. Queen Victoria had doubtless been on the throne when the doorknob had been fixed into position, and Tom King and Jem Mace were doubtless contesting the English Bare Knuckle Boxing Championships.

There were no visible signs that the knob had ever been moved, amended or even fiddled with during the century that it had been in situ.

I bent down and wiggled the knob.

It was quickly clear that it had become loose because one of the two screws which should have held it in position had come loose. It was so loose that it fell on the floor when I jiggled the knob. I picked up the screw. It looked as if it had been hand carved by a skilled 19th century artisan. I wondered, idly, if they had screw making machines in those distant days or if patient workmen produced the things one at a time in an atelier in Clerkenwell or some forgotten corner of Wolverhampton.

I put the screw back into the hole from which it had fallen, picked out a suitable screwdriver, and tried to tighten it.

It just went round and round.

It seemed that the hole into which it had originally been secured had, for some bizarre reason of its own, expanded and become too spacious for the screw which had been doing a difficult and important job calmly and without fuss for a century or more.

I undid the other screw and removed it. The doorknob now came off in my hand, leaving just a spindle behind.

I was staring at the loose knob wondering how I could fasten it more securely and wondering if filling the screw hole with glue would do the trick, when Patsy returned.

'It's Ethel Fairfield,' she told me, rather wearily. 'She says she needs you to go round to see her.'

'Did she say what was wrong?'

'She wouldn't tell me,' replied Patsy. 'She just said that she wants you to visit and that what she needs can't be dealt with at the evening surgery.'

I sighed and put the doorknob down on the floor.

Mrs Fairfield is, I'm afraid, a rather difficult patient.

She genuinely enjoys poor health and enjoys it far more than anyone else I've ever known.

A very distinguished 19th century French neurologist called Jean-Martin Charcot, who was one of the world's pioneering neurologists and, as though that were not enough, also a professor of anatomical pathology, described patients who have a long list of signs, symptoms and ill-defined complaints as suffering from 'le maladie du petit papier'.

The name was well chosen since, in addition to requiring their doctor to maintain a massive medical record, most such patients bring with them a long list of their problems.

As I have explained before, it is a traditional medical practice, and a primary tenet of good diagnosis, to try to find a single disease to explain all of a patient's health problems. But it has to be said that with patients such as Mrs Fairfield this is rarely, if ever possible.

In addition to her wealth of ill-defined illnesses, Mrs Fairfield enjoys and wallows in the injustices of fate. She clutches every misery she can find to her bosom with great enthusiasm. She loves the attention and the sympathy that she gets and as a result she considers a day without disasters, disappointments and frustrations to be a wasted day. On those rare occasions when she cannot easily locate a source of anguish, she will do everything she can to find one or, preferably, two.

'The knob has come loose,' I told Patsy, quite unnecessarily. Since it was on the floor at the time this was a considerable understatement.

My wife did not seem surprised by this. Indeed, it had been Patsy who had originally drawn my attention to the problem.

'Ah,' she said, nodding wisely. 'Do you have a remedy to go with the diagnosis?'

'I do!' I said, proudly.

She could not have appeared more impressed if I had announced that I'd managed to find a way to split an atom with nothing more than a soup spoon and a nutcracker.

'One of the screws has fallen out,' I explained. 'So I thought I might try filling the hole with glue and then putting the screw back into place.'

'Ah,' said Patsy.

I felt that she did not seem as impressed by the specifics of my proposal as she had been by the generality, when the plan had been nothing more than a promise.

'Or I could move the knob round so that both the screws go into fresh wood.' I suggested. I looked at the spindle. 'I really don't think we want to fiddle around with the lock. It looks a bit complicated.'

'We definitely don't want to fiddle around with the lock,' said Patsy, quite firmly. 'That's definitely not an option.'

'We could just leave the knob off and use my plier thingies to turn the spindle if we wanted to open the door from this side,' I suggested. I tentatively tried gripping the spindle with my plier thingies. It wasn't as easy as I had thought it ought to be. 'We could keep the plier thingies on this shelf so that they were always handy.'

Patsy did not look too thrilled by this suggestion. She has, in the past, accused me of being something of a 'bodger' when it comes to doing chores around the house. I think this probably stems from the time when I glued a piece of glass taken from a picture frame over a large crack in a window pane in the kitchen. My claim that this would act as an area of double-glazing, and therefore preserve heat during the colder months, did not seem convincing even to me. When I start looking for quick, easy solutions to complicated problems she calls me Mr Bodger.

(This reminds me of a time when I asked Thumper for the name of a plumber who would be able to deal with a small problem in

Bilbury Grange without re-plumbing the whole house. 'I know just the fellow,' said Thumper, scribbling a phone number down on a scrap of paper. 'Call old Bodgett. He'll sort you out.' I duly rang the number and asked to speak to Mr Bodgett. Unfortunately, the man's name was Birkenshaw. He was not amused by the nickname he had been given. Indeed, he was so not amused that he refused to come out and deal with our problem. He even rang several of his colleagues and told them not to do any work for us. Thumper thought the whole thing was hilarious.)

'Then, when we get fed up with using the plier thingies to open the door, we could ring someone up and ask a professional to take a look.'

'That's a very good idea,' said Patsy, who has never made any secret of the fact that she believes that all do-it-yourself chores around the house are best tackled by professionals.

'But who?' I asked. 'Do we need to call the carpenter or the locksmith?'

Patsy looked at me and frowned. 'I doubt if it matters terribly much,' she said. 'But meanwhile, you'd better get off and see what Mrs Fairfield wants.'

Mrs Fairfield lives in a neat, thatched cottage no more than a mile away from Bilbury Grange and I have visited her so often that I suspect that, if I had a little more faith, the car would take me there by itself if I just told it to take me round to Mrs Fairfield.

When my predecessor, Dr Brownlow, first started in practice, he did his rounds and visits on horseback and he once told me that his horse knew the locations of his most regular patients so well that on getting onto his horse's back, or into the dogcart, he claimed that he simply had to say the patient's name and then sit back and wait to be taken to his destination.

I didn't believe this but Dr Brownlow's former butler, who is now the practise nurse and matron of the Brownlow Country Hotel, insists that the tale was true.

Mrs Fairfield is a woman who probably regards the word 'unfashionable' as a compliment. Her cottage is furnished in such a way that if a Victorian of either sex were ever transported by time machine to the 1970s and, by chance, found him or herself a guest of Mrs Fairfield, he or she would feel very much at home.

Like many ladies of her age she still eschews electricity, which she regards as an untrustworthy modern invention. She says that we may consider her old-fashioned but insists that in due course, when we have all been blown up or poisoned by allowing electricity into our homes, we will wish we too had refused to allow the electricity board to fill our homes with wiring. She has a telephone, but no electrical appliances.

Her home is lit by paraffin lamps and heated by a coal fire in the drawing room. She cooks on a huge four oven coal fired AGA which dominates her kitchen. After a couple of glasses of sherry she once told me that she regarded electricity as being nothing more than the work of the devil. This may sound strange to those who live in towns and cities but it is not an uncommon view in North Devon.

When I first told my medical friend Will that many of the patients I look after live in homes without electricity he, like our other friends who live in towns and cities where street lighting is commonplace, was astonished. 'But this is the 1970s!' he said. 'I didn't think anyone lived in a house without electricity!'

One day, when he and his family were having a short holiday in Bilbury, I took him round to see Mrs Fairfield.

He was, he admitted, utterly enchanted by seeing a cottage lit by lamps and heated by an open fire and he later admitted that he thought it would be dangerous if he ever practised in my part of the world.

'To my astonishment, I sympathise with your eccentric patients,' he confessed. 'I rather envy their old-fashioned lifestyle and I fear I could quite easily adopt some of their suspicions and fears – particularly the one regarding electricity.'

He said he could cope very well without television or telephone answering machines and I do not think he was joking.

I noted, however, that he did not tell his wife of his secret affection for a 19th century lifestyle. I think he knew that she would not be keen to give up modern appliances such as the washing machine and vacuum cleaner.

'Ah, do come in doctor,' said Mrs Fairfield when she opened the door of her cottage. She was wearing a pink gingham frock with lots of stiff petticoats and had her hair in side bunches. She looked as if she had been dressed by the costume designer for a local dramatic society trying to find a 'look' for a 1950s teenage girl. Mrs Fairfield hadn't been a teenager since the 1930s.

I know she saw me arrive because I can always see her peering out through the net curtains but she never opens the door until I use the big, solid, iron knocker (which is made out of a shire horse's shoe). I think this is partly because she doesn't want me to know that she has been spying through the net curtains and partly because she thinks it rather improper to open the door until a caller has knocked upon it.

She led me into her drawing room and invited me to sit down. 'Would you like a glass of sherry?' she asked.

I politely declined, explaining that I was driving and that the authorities were now taking a dim view of drivers who drank alcohol.

'Oh, that's so silly,' she said. 'My father wouldn't drive his car unless he had drunk at least half a bottle of port. He said the car did 15 miles to the gallon and he did the same to the half a bottle of port.' She always told me this and I suspect that she was being honest. What she didn't mention was that as a result of his affection for port, her father suffered terribly from gout and spent the last decade of his life in an old-fashioned bath-chair, unable to walk more than a couple of yards because of badly swollen big toes. I remember him well. He had a very old set of the *Encyclopaedia Britannica*, which he claimed to have read from Aard-vark to zymurgy and, as a result, he liked to think of himself as something of an intellectual. When I first met him he described himself as a 'suppository of wisdom'.

Ignoring my refusal, which she seemed to regard as of no consequence and nothing more than a sign of a good upbringing, Mrs Fairfield poured me a large dose of sherry, using a schooner glass that would have been more appropriate for beer than for wine of any description. In Britain, a schooner is a large sherry glass but at some point in her life Mrs Fairfield had been given a set of half a dozen Australian schooners, designed for beer, and she had confused the British measure with the Australian one. When she wasn't looking, I would always pour my half pint or so of sherry into a large earthenware pot which contained an aspidistra plant. The aspidistra clearly loved sherry for it was the healthiest plant in the village. If you sat within a yard of it you could smell alcohol. I think that Mrs

Fairfield probably thought that all aspidistra plants smelt of sherry. This ritual followed the same pattern every time I visited.

'What can I do for you?' I asked her.

'I need you to turn my mattress,' said Mrs Fairfield. 'I bought a new mattress three months ago and the man who delivered it said that I should have it turned every three months.'

I looked at her, not quite sure what to say.

I have, in my life, been asked to do many strange things. I've helped a patient build a lawnmower (my contribution consisted mostly of holding nuts and bolts and cursing myself when I dropped them in the long grass). I have cut a budgerigar's claws. I have driven a patient to the railway station. I have helped to extricate a cat trapped behind an oil tank. And I have liberated a mouse from inside a radiator. But I had never before turned a mattress.

'It's gone a little saggy on one side,' said Mrs Fairfield, when she had led me upstairs, peeled back the bedclothes and moved a surprisingly skimpy satin nightdress from the pillow.

What she said was absolutely true.

One side of the bed looked as though it had long been the nocturnal resting place for one of the larger mammals, a hippopotamus or a rhinoceros for example.

'Couldn't you simply sleep on the other side of the bed for a while?'

'Oh no, certainly not,' said Mrs Fairfield, quite shocked. 'That was always my husband's side of the bed. I have always slept on the left side of the bed.'

Mrs Fairfield has been a widow for several years. Her husband died of a heart attack while still quite young. He was fond of food, a gourmand rather than a gourmet, and after his untimely demise, he had to be moved out of the house through an upstairs window because his corpse proved to be far too large to manoeuvre up and down the narrow staircase. Heaven knows how he had managed to get himself up and down the stairs when he had been alive.

Patsy's father loaned and manipulated a tractor with a forklift attachment and while Mrs Fairfield was distracted and comforted at a neighbour's house, her erstwhile spouse was pushed and shoved onto a pallet placed upon the two forks, lowered out of the bedroom window and transferred to the back of one of Mr Kennet's trailers.

The problems didn't end there.

Poor Mr Fairfield was too big to fit inside the undertaker's hearse.

The undertaker had covered him with a tarpaulin and the late Mr Fairfield had been transferred to his premises on Mr Kennet's tractor. At the workshop behind the funeral home, a suitably extensive coffin had been built around him.

I don't think we have more than our fair share of deaths in Bilbury but we certainly have more than our fair share of trouble with bodies and coffins. There was, I remember, one incident when a coffin ended up being washed down a river during a storm.

'Have you thought about investing in a new mattress?' I asked her.

'This is a new mattress!' said Mrs Fairfield. 'I bought it last year. Peter Marshall ordered it in especially for me. It was made by a company which makes mattresses for royalty.' She pulled back the sheet and proudly showed me a label which contained the crest of a European monarch I did not know existed. 'It came in a very large lorry,' she announced, as if this gave the mattress extra kudos. 'A pantechnicon I think they call them. The lorry was so big that the driver got stuck and the road past the Duck and Puddle was blocked for several hours.'

I remembered the incident well. Thumper, Patchy and I had been having lunch when the vehicle had got stuck. The driver, exhausted and bad tempered by his attempts to persuade his vehicle to go round a corner designed for dog carts and pony traps, had come into the pub for a break. As a result of the vehicle being stuck Thumper, Patchy and I had been trapped and stranded and had had to remain in the bar far longer than we had intended.

After some lubrication, the driver had succeeded in extricating his vehicle. He had then parked it in a ditch and gone to sleep.

It was two days later when the now sober but also embarrassed driver had finally left the village, aided by two breakdown trucks and Mr Kennet's second best tractor.

I lifted one corner of the mattress. It seemed very heavy. In my experience, mattresses are always heavier and more cumbersome than you think they ought to be.

'I'm not really sure that moving mattresses around is part of my job as your GP,' I said hesitantly.

Mrs Fairfield stared at me, as though I'd made an indecent remark or an improper suggestion.

'Good heavens, doctor!' she said. 'I am surprised at you. I always thought of you as a friend.' She paused. 'Besides,' she continued, 'I have a bad back. If the mattress isn't just right then my back will give me a lot of trouble. I thought you doctors were very keen on preventative medicine. Isn't it supposed to be the 'in-thing' these days?'

I know when I'm defeated; outflanked, out manoeuvred and out gunned.

I bent down and removed the sheets from the bed. The mattress was equipped with two handles on each side. I took hold of the two handles nearest to me and lifted. Just raising the mattress a foot off the base took an enormous effort. I let go and the mattress thumped back onto the base.

'You'll have to do better than that!' said Mrs Fairfield. 'It's only a mattress!'

'It's a very big mattress,' I pointed out.

'It's called a king size,' said Mrs Fairfield proudly, 'though Mr Marshall said that may be because of the endorsement.' She pointed to the label with the royal crest.

'I think 'king size' is just one of the sizes they make,' I said, though you could write what I know about mattresses on a crumbly aspirin tablet.

I made another attempt to lift the mattress. This time I managed to lift the mattress several feet into the air. I dragged it towards me and then raised it to a vertical position. It was very heavy. I have not done a great deal of mattress turning in my life, it has never been a speciality of mine, but I remembered, at that moment, that it is terribly easy, while wrestling with a mattress, to become confused and to forget which way the mattress was lying when you started out. It is perfectly possible to move a mattress about on a bed and get so confused that you end up with it back in exactly the same place it was when the whole business started.

'You need to turn it round and over,' said Mrs Fairfield. 'You must make sure that the bottom is at the top and the top is at the bottom and the left is on the right and the...'

'...and the right is on the left,' I finished.

'And be careful of the bedside tables,' said Mrs Fairfield. 'I don't want them damaging.'

'Of course,' I said.

'And the light shade. It's very close to the top of the mattress, the way you've got it at the moment.'

I closed my eyes and tried to summon up my energy for the next part of the procedure. I remembered her late husband, Mr Fairfield, was a smoker and was known to have bitten through the stems of seven or eight pipes. When questioned about this, Mrs Fairfield always insisted that he bit through his pipe stems because he had a bad temper and used to get very angry. But I never believed her. Mr Fairfield himself told me that he used to bite his pipe whenever his wife annoyed him with one of her silly sayings or opinions. If that had truly been the case then I'm surprised that he only bit through seven or eight pipes.

'I long ago learned not to argue with her,' he told me in a rare moment of candour. 'I usually just keep quiet. I only ever bite through my pipe when I feel an almost overwhelming desire to strangle her.'

Mrs Fairfield said that Mr Fairfield died of an excess of prejudices and too much impatience but I always suspected that in truth her husband died of too much tolerance and a great desire to avoid confrontation. It was suppressing his feelings that did the damage. If he'd shouted occasionally, or thrown some crockery from time to time, he might have lived a little longer.

Of course, weighing slightly north of 30 stone didn't help much.

I always remembered him with great understanding and some fondness.

I remember that he had on several occasions tried to lose weight. He had once gone to a hotel for a month. 'The food there is terrible,' he told me, 'I thought that if I went somewhere with rotten food I'd be bound to lose some weight.'

But it hadn't worked.

He had come back weighing half a stone more than he'd weighed when he'd left home. It turned out that he had persuaded the hotel chef to serve him a cooked breakfast three times a day. Huge piles of sausages, bacon, fried eggs, grilled tomatoes, baked beans and fried bread had done the damage.

I had pretended to be cross with him but what can you do with someone who thinks up such a sure fire plan for losing weight and then thinks up a sure fire plan for getting round it?

Inch by inch I pulled the mattress across the bed towards me. I wondered why they hadn't included 'mattress turning' in the medical school curriculum. It was becoming clear my medical education had been sadly lacking in a number of areas.

'I see that Mrs Oswald is having trouble with her knees again,' said Mrs Fairfield. 'She has a lot of trouble with them. I've told her that you won't be able to help her and she should go and see my osteopath in Taunton.'

'That's very kind of you,' I said, through gritted teeth. I fervently wished I had a pipe to bite through. The mattress, standing upright, was now balanced almost on the edge of the bed.

'Professor Entwhistle, that's my osteopath, has a wonderful manner,' said Mrs Fairfield. 'And he's a very talented man. He has many diplomas in frames on his consulting room wall. He's cured many patients.'

'Hmph,' I said, still clutching the mattress. I was beginning to perspire and wished I'd taken off my jacket. Actually, I was beginning to wish I'd had the telephone disconnected. Or maybe I should have taken that job as a ship's doctor that I'd seen advertised in the *British Medical Journal*. Patsy could have come with me and we could have sailed around the world. I was pretty sure that no ship's doctor would be expected to turn a mattress.

'He's been so successful that you people are always trying to shut him down,' said Mrs Fairfield. 'It's just jealousy, of course. I really think you should leave him alone.'

'I haven't done anything to him,' I gasped. 'I don't even know the fellow.'

'You people are always saying bad things about him,' said Mrs Fairfield. 'You doctors and the police.'

'The police?'

'That business with the young girl was wildly exaggerated,' said Mrs Fairfield. 'Professor Entwhistle told me the truth about that. And the pills from Mexico are perfectly legal in Mexico so I can't see why he should get into so much trouble for prescribing them over here.'

I muttered something and tried to scratch my nose which was itching.

'I hear that Frank is dying,' she said. 'It's just a matter of time now. Poor Gilly.'

107

'Frank Parsons? At the Duck and Puddle?'

'Yes.'

'Where on earth did you hear that?' I demanded, rather crossly. 'He's doing very well.'

'Oh,' said Mrs Fairfield. She actually sounded disappointed.

'Don't just let it flop down,' said Mrs Fairfield. 'You'll make a lot of dust if you do. My cleaner came in to clean yesterday and she did this room from top to bottom.'

It suddenly occurred to me to wonder why, since Mr Fairfield had been dead for quite a while, the fairly new mattress had acquired such a huge dip in one side. Mrs Fairfield looked to weigh no more than a hungry sparrow. Who had been sleeping on that side of the bed? Why wasn't he moving the damned mattress? It was his fault it had a dip in it.

I tried to lower the mattress steadily but suddenly found that as the mattress fell, it was taking me with it. The mattress landed back on the base with a crash, with me lying on top of it. Any remaining dignity I had brought with me when I had arrived had now evaporated.

'Where's Fluffy?' demanded Mrs Fairfield suddenly.

'Fluffy?' I asked.

'My Pekinese,' explained Mrs Fairfield, her voice raising towards the sort of level associated with hysteria. 'Have you crushed him? You have, haven't you? You've killed Fluffy!'

I scrambled off the mattress as quickly as I could, lifted it a little and peered underneath. To my intense relief there were no crushed dogs to be seen. I looked for Mrs Fairfield to give her the good news but she had disappeared. I wondered idly if crushing a dog while moving a mattress was an offence for which I could have been struck off the medical register. I thought that, on balance, I would probably get away with it since it would have been a first offence.

I was now beginning to lose the plot.

I was pretty certain that I had succeeded in turning the mattress so that the top was now the bottom and the bottom now the top. I looked for the label with the royal crest. It was nowhere to be seen. I was therefore satisfied that part one of the operation had been completed successfully. All I had to do now was turn the mattress so that the part which had been next to the headboard was at the other end of the base. If I could manage that then I was pretty certain that the bottom end of the bed would end up at the headboard end.

I regretted, for the first time that I could remember, that I hadn't done much mattress turning in my life. It is not a subject in which I have ever shown any real interest or for which I have ever felt any enthusiasm.

I pulled at the mattress and with considerable difficulty, succeeded in moving it around the bed. On reflection, I suppose that the collision with one of the bedside tables was inevitable. The mattress was large and heavy and the bedside tables were relatively light and well stocked with delicate, fragile objets d'art.

Fortunately, the crash was not a particularly noisy one since the falling object landed onto a thick pile carpet. I put the two largest pieces of the broken model lighthouse under the bed. It was cream, a hideous piece of 1950s kitsch, and had the words 'A Present from Cornwall' inscribed around the base. I hoped that its very hideousness did not make it unique and irreplaceable.

'He was hiding underneath the sofa,' said Mrs Fairfield, returning with a smug looking Pekinese.

'That's a relief,' I said. No one wants to squash a dog while turning a mattress. I kicked another piece of the broken lighthouse under the bed.

Mrs Fairfield ignored me but the dog barked.

'Did the nasty man frighten you?' she asked the dog. It somehow managed to look smugger than ever.

'I think that's it,' I said, standing up and feeling my back. I was soaked with sweat and ached in every muscle. 'Do you need anything else doing while I'm here? Lawn mowing? Roof rethatching? A bit of ironing, perhaps? Maybe I could clean the windows or service the washing machine.'

I didn't say any of the last bit, of course. Perhaps I should have done. Would Dr Brownlow have moved the damned mattress? I'm pretty sure he wouldn't. Actually, Mrs Fairfield wouldn't have dared ask him. It occurred to me that I needed to acquire a little more gravitas. But how did one do that? I had been in the village for a while now. I had a wife, a family, a pig and lots of friends. What else did I need? I decided that perhaps I ought to start wearing a waistcoat and sporting a pince nez.

'There was a telephone call for you,' said Mrs Fairfield.

I thought she might have said thank you. But she didn't. She wasn't the sort of person who ever said 'thank you'.

'For me?'

'Your wife called.'

'Why didn't you tell me?' I asked. 'It might be urgent.'

'You were turning the mattress,' said Mrs Fairfield. 'I told your wife you couldn't come to the telephone.'

'Do you mind if I call her back?' I asked, biting my tongue and trying not to show how cross I was.

Mrs Fairfield pursed her lips. 'Since it's just a local call I suppose it will be all right.'

I rang Bilbury Grange from Mrs Fairfield's telephone. Like most people in Bilbury she has just one extension, and a telephone which sat in her hallway, on a little table with a chair next to it. Only the wealthiest have a second telephone in their bedroom. (Patsy and I do not class as wealthy by any means but we have a telephone in our bedroom for obvious, practical reasons.)

'What on earth is going on?' asked Patsy stifling a giggle. 'Mrs Fairfield said you were busy in her bedroom.'

'I'll tell you when I see you.'

'What on earth were doing in her bedroom when she clearly wasn't in her bedroom?' asked Patsy, clearly puzzled.

'It's a bit complicated,' I said. To be honest I didn't want to admit that I'd been turning Mrs Fairfield's mattress. It didn't really sound very professional. I wasn't even sure how I'd got tricked into doing it in the first place.

'Mrs Fresnel rang,' said Patsy. 'She wondered if you'd pop in. I thought you could go there on your way back.'

'I'm leaving now,' I said. 'I should be home soon. Then I'll have a cup of tea, change my shirt and then finish that doorknob.'

'Change your shirt?'

'I got a little sweaty.'

'In Mrs Fairfield's bedroom?'

'Exactly.'

There was a silence. 'I look forward to hearing about it when you get back,' said Patsy, suppressing another giggle.

We said goodbye and I put down the receiver.

As I got to the front door it opened and a huge figure appeared in the doorway. The figure was Bill Blake, one of Mr Kennet's labourers. Bill is about six foot six inches tall and built like a stone statue of Goliath and just as no one ever calls Mrs Fairfield 'Ethel' so no one ever addresses 'Bill' by his surname. He is vast and can never find clothes to fit him. Thumper once said that the only suit that has ever fitted him properly was the one he was born in. A couple of years ago, I had to examine Bill for a medical and found to our mutual embarrassment that I could not weigh him because my surgery scales only measure up to 20 stone. He must weigh at least three times as much as Mrs Fairfield. He is a pleasant fellow but a genuinely clumsy man who always looks as though he got dressed in the dark. Buttons are always in the wrong holes and socks never match. He smelt, as he always does, of a cheap aftershave but underneath that there was a strong, lingering smell of silage and manure. I suspect that Bill always smelt of silage and manure in the same way that trawler-men always smell of a mixture of diesel oil and fish.

'Hello, doctor!' he said. 'What are you doing here?'

He seemed a little embarrassed.

I couldn't think why and then I suddenly remembered that he had been to the surgery a couple of weeks earlier.

He had ostensibly turned up to ask for something for a slightly sore back. This had surprised me because Bill is a tough fellow who, like most farm labourers, won't ask for medical advice unless a limb is actually hanging off.

On his way out of the surgery, with his hand actually on the doorknob, he had turned to ask if I could put his mind at rest about something relating to his sex life. This had clearly been the main reason for his visiting the surgery.

'The lady I'm with has quite unusual demands,' he told me, blushing bright red. I'd asked him to sit down again and he'd confessed that although the new lady in his life (he had named no names) had expressed no dissatisfaction with the size of equipment on offer, or the quality of the performance provided, she had rather startled him by her activities in the bedroom and one or two of the requests had caused him some concern.

It was clear from what he said that she knew a few tricks which he had never come across before. He had been delighted and relieved when I had assured him that the activities in question were commonplace and that the positions he was being required to favour were by no means exceptional.

'The doctor came to turn the mattress,' said Mrs Fairfield. I was, I confess, delighted to see that it was now her turn to go bright red.

Bill's appearance had clearly been slightly unexpected.

I realised now why half of Mrs Fairfield's mattress had a dip in it. To say that Bill is huge is like saying that the Sahara desert is sandy.

Mrs Fairfield and Bill Blake seemed an unlikely couple. I couldn't help smiling to myself. It seemed that Mrs Fairfield had a penchant for large men.

'Hello Bill,' I said. 'I've not seen you for ages. How are you?'

He looked greatly relieved at my tactful and anodyne remark. We exchanged greetings as though we had not seen each other for some considerable time. Tact, trust and discretion are vital parts of a GP's daily armoury. It saddens me to know that many people want to chip away at doctor-patient confidentiality. Politicians, policemen and even some senior members of the medical establishment believe that doctors should spill the beans on their patients' activities whenever required to do so. I suspect that they will eventually get their way. Meanwhile, I'm glad that I'm practising in the 1970s. I hope that my medical career will be over by the time it becomes illegal for doctors to regard patient confidentiality as sacrosanct.

'You should have said about the mattress,' said Bill to Mrs Fairfield. 'I could have done that for you. No need to have bothered the doctor.'

'I didn't like to ask you, dear,' said Mrs Fairfield. 'It's not the sort of job for a man like you.'

I thought it was actually very much the sort of job for a man like Bill. He could probably pick up a mattress with one hand, twirl it over his head, turn it over and throw it back onto the bed while holding a cup of tea in his other hand.

Without another word, Bill strode into the house, squeezed past us both and marched up the stairs. 'I'll do the mattress,' he said.

Slightly startled, Mrs Fairfield watched him go upstairs but did not say anything.

'It's OK, I've done it,' I called after him. But Bill didn't hear me. He's always been slightly deaf. He drives a very noisy tractor and it has, over the years, affected his hearing. One day, someone in authority is going to have to suggest that men who drive tractors and other noisy machinery need to wear ear defenders.

'We met at a Church picnic last summer,' said Mrs Fairfield, though I had not asked for any explanation. 'He saved me from a creepy crawly.'

There was the sound of strenuous activity in the bedroom.

'Ah,' I said.

'It was sitting on a piece of Mrs Butterworth's apricot flan.'

A moment or two later Bill appeared at the top of the stairs. 'I've done it!' he called down. 'I've turned it upside down and top to bottom.'

'Thank you, dear,' said Mrs Fairfield.

Bill had, I realised, put the mattress back where it had been before I'd started. I don't think Mrs Fairfield realised quite what had happened.

I said goodbye to Mrs Fairfield, shouted goodbye to Bill and left. I didn't like to say anything about the mattress.

The visit to Mrs Fairfield had taken well over an hour but the call on Mrs Fresnel took only three or four minutes. She wanted another prescription for a bottle of the tonic I give her. The bottle contains absolutely nothing with pharmacological qualities but it is green, tastes rather bitter and is in Mrs Fresnel's view the most important development in pharmacology since Fleming discovered penicillin.

Since she is the patient and the 'Mixture' which I prescribe and dispense keeps her well and happy, I will not hear a word said against it.

As I approached Bilbury Grange, I remembered the darned doorknob. I wasn't looking forward to trying to fix it.

'I've got some crumpets,' said Patsy when I had taken off my shoes. 'If I toast a few how many could you eat?'

'Dripping with butter?'

'Of course.'

'Three?' I suggested. 'Would three be greedy?'

'Not at all,' replied Patsy.

'I'll have three, then.'

And then I remembered the doorknob.

'I suppose I'd better do the doorknob first,' I said, feeling sorry for myself. My day seemed to be made up of doorknobs and mattresses.

'Oh, that's done,' said Patsy dismissively.

'Done? Who did it?'

'I did it,' said Patsy with a modest grin.

'How…?'

'I just used longer screws,' she replied. 'I'll put the crumpets under the grill.'

The toaster may do both sides at once but crumpets never taste the same as when they have been toasted under the grill. Besides, our toaster seems to have been designed by a former aerospace engineer. When it has finished toasting it throws the toast upwards with the velocity of a V2 rocket. Unless I stand near enough to catch the toasted bread as it flies out it usually ends up on the floor.

'No, not the grill,' I said. 'I'll do them on the fire. That was brilliant! Mending the door like that.'

'I know.'

I went and checked the door. The knob worked perfectly and seemed as solid as a doorknob should be.

'You're marvellous!' I said to her.

'I couldn't have done it with you,' she said with a mischievous smile.

I'd have chased her round the kitchen if I hadn't been so exhausted.

'Next time I'll stick to holding the sticking plasters and the antiseptic,' I suggested.

'I think that would be a good idea,' said Patsy brightly. 'It's what you do best.

I took a plateful of crumpets into the living room and skewered one on the end of our extendable brass toasting fork.

Crumpets may taste better when toasted on the grill then they do when browned in the toaster but they taste better still when prepared on an open fire. And for that you need a long handled, preferably extendable, toasting fork. Anything, crumpets, pikelets or bread, smells and tastes so much better when prepared on a real fire. It's true that some bits get burnt, and it's true that you're likely to burn a finger or two as well. But none of that matters for crumpets, toasted on a real, log fire, are every bit as much a part of England as are costermongers and knife grinders, curds and whey, pecks and bushels and Toby jugs and singing glasses.

Patsy came carrying a wooden tray upon which she had placed a teapot, a tea strainer, a milk jug, a sugar bowl, two cups and two saucers, two plates, two knives and a butter dish.

'What sort of tea have you made?' I asked.

'Lapsang souchong,' replied Patsy.

Bliss. A heavenly repast: slightly burnt crumpets, generously buttered, and a cup of lapsang souchong – the only tea which smells of bonfire. Ambrosia never tasted half as good and the Greek Gods never knew such glories.

'Now are you going to tell me how you got sweaty in Mrs Fairfield's bedroom?' asked Patsy, putting the tray on a small table and settling herself in one of a pair of old and comfortable easy chairs beside the fireplace. A cat immediately jumped up onto her lap.

'I think I can do that,' I said. 'I don't think the principles of medical confidentiality are relevant in this particular case.' We both take patient confidentiality very seriously. Some doctors will talk to their family and friends about their patients. I have never felt comfortable doing that. Both Patsy and I feel easier if I regard the sanctity of the consulting room as inviolable. Besides, it is easier for Patsy if she can talk to villagers without knowing things she isn't supposed to know.

'Oh good,' said Patsy. 'That will save me the effort of attacking you with a red hot toasting fork.'

It's a long and complicated story,' I said, changing the toasting fork from my right hand to my left because my fingers were beginning to get rather hot.

'Splendid,' said Patsy, with a sigh of contentment. 'I like long and complicated stories.'

'You may, or may not, know but Mrs Fairfield has a large and saggy mattress…' I began.

And for some inexplicable reason Patsy started to laugh.

I looked at her sternly. 'You may well laugh,' I admonished her. 'But Mrs Fairfield didn't find her saggy mattress in the slightest bit amusing.' I checked on the crumpet I was toasting. It needed another minute. 'The basic problem was that the mattress was only half saggy…

A Trip to the Farrier

I got up one morning and discovered that both constituent halves of my favourite pair of brown brogue shoes were coming apart. The sole on one shoe flapped as I walked, making me look rather like a circus clown, and the sole on the other was, when I took a close look, also clinging onto the upper part of the shoe without much hope of staying in close contact for very much longer. This had clearly happened overnight.

'You need to get that mended,' said Patsy, when she saw me flapping my way along the hall, heading for the front door, the car and my morning visits. 'Haven't you got another pair you could wear today?'

I do not own a large collection of shoes.

I have a brown pair and a black pair. That woman from the Philippines, the one with the impressive footwear collection, would not find my morning shoe choice satisfactory. I tend to find a pair of shoes which I like, and which are comfortable, and then to wear them until they fall apart. 'My black shoes have a hole in the sole,' I said. 'They're in an even worse state than these.'

'Haven't you got anything else you could wear?'

'The choice is between a pair of Wellington boots or a pair of rather down at heel slippers,' I told her. 'I'll have to wear these until I can get into Barnstaple and go to the cobbler's.'

This was not a thought which filled me with delight. I couldn't for the life of me remember the location of a shoe repairer in Barnstaple.

But I did remember my last attempt to find one.

'Go down past the old church,' said an old man whom I asked for directions. 'It's either St John's or St Marks; one or the other. Then cross the road by the Post Office, well what used to be the Post Office, I think it's a pet shop now. Take the first right after the laundry, though I think it might have been turned into a Chinese takeaway, and go down a little alley which leads to the Bowchester warehouse which was converted into a nightclub two or three years ago. Anyway, go down the alley unless it's blocked with garbage bins which it sometimes is, and when you get to the end you'll see the traffic lights. There's a baker's on the corner. It's a video shop now, I think. Go straight across, but a bit to your right, and you'll see Cross Street or Croft Street, one of the two, and when you get to the end you'll see where the old bus station was. Go right where the old bus station used to be and walk along the bank of the estuary and look for a right hand turn that has a pub on the left hand side, the Duke's Head or the Swan's Nest I think it is. Then take the third or fourth turning on the left and look for a narrow road that needs repairing. There used to be an optician somewhere down there but it closed. I don't think anyone could ever find it. Go about a hundred and fifty yards up that road and there are three shops in a row. I think one of those is the cobbler's. No, I tell a lie. I think they closed that down too. I think they knocked down all three shops and built some flats.'

Is it only me who meets people like that?

Is it any wonder that I am always reluctant to stop and ask for directions?

Suddenly, I realised that Patsy had said something.

'I'm sorry,' I said, 'I was day dreaming. What did you say?'

'Go and see Albert Ross,' said Patsy. 'He'll repair them for you.'

I looked at her, puzzled. 'But Albert is a farrier,' I said. 'He puts shoes on horses and makes iron gates as a side line.'

'He'll mend your shoes,' insisted Patsy. 'He's been mending my Dad's shoes for years.'

'I'd feel embarrassed, asking a farrier to mend my shoes,' I said.

'Don't be silly!' laughed Patsy. 'He mends a lot of shoes. He won't mind. And he'll only charge you a pound a pair. Take the black ones with you.' She opened the hall cupboard where we keep boots and shoes and rummaged around among tennis rackets, umbrellas, walking sticks, miscellaneous old boxes, bits and pieces that looked as if they probably fitted a vacuum cleaner we have never owned and a variety of shopping bags. As she buried deeper into the cupboard I could not help noticing that none of the things in the cupboard is ever used.

'Why do we keep all that junk?' I asked her.

'You never know,' Patsy replied, from deep inside the cupboard. 'If we throw anything away then tomorrow we'll find that we need it.'

I knew she was right.

Suddenly Patsy emerged from the dark of the cupboard holding first one and then the other black shoe aloft in mock triumph.

'We must get someone in to fit a light in that cupboard,' she said.

'If I had the skill and the tools I could probably do it myself.'

She looked at me.

'Sorry. I'll ask the electrician to put a light in.'

We both knew that I wouldn't and that the cupboard would remain darkened. There are a dozen jobs around the house which need doing but somehow I always manage to put off doing anything about them. I mean to get things mended, repaired or improved but there are always other things which need doing. Finding a tradesman able to turn up on the approximate date and do the work he's been invited to do, seems to become more difficult by the year. There are, however, some tasks I can manage by myself. Sitting in the garden, for example, seems to take up an increasing amount of my time in the summer months. That is something I can cope with perfectly well by myself.

'Do you know where Albert lives?' asked Patsy.

'Turn left a quarter of mile after Softly's Bottom, then take the lane on the right and the second track on the left,' I said. 'There's a dead elm just on the corner and two huge ruts running all the way along the track.' I was proud of my knowledge of the geography of Bilbury and the surrounding district and sometimes I liked to show off a little. Patsy had lived in the village all her life but even she admitted that I knew my way around Bilbury even better than she did. 'I'll call in to see him when I've done the morning calls.'

'And don't forget to take these with you,' she said, handing me the pair of black shoes that needed repairing. I took the shoes, flapped my way along the hall, still in the style of a circus clown with size 18 boots, climbed into the Rolls and drove off to do the morning visits.

As luck would have it, I left the Bilbury Grange driveway just as a tourist was driving past. I know most of the local vehicles and I always dread being caught behind a car being driven by a tourist driving along our narrow, one car width, country lanes. Most occasional visitors find it difficult to get used to driving along narrow lanes which have grass growing through the tarmacadam in the middle of them and brambles hanging over the road at the sides. As a result, they tend to drive at the sort of speed favoured by the men who drive undertakers' hearses for a living. Thumper once pointed out that he regards people who drive slower than him as idiots and people who drive faster than he does as lunatics. I can see the sense in that.

Still, I eventually got where I was heading.

And, just as importantly, I managed to do so without allowing my blood pressure to rise to dangerous levels. I did this by singing an aria from the Barber of Seville. I didn't know many of the words and I wasn't terribly sure of the tune but since I can't sing and am pretty well tone-deaf none of that mattered terribly much. I entertained myself, aired my lungs and kept my stress levels down to acceptable levels.

(If I want music in the Rolls, I have to provide it myself. In the days when our Rolls was manufactured, in-car entertainment was confined to counting the pimples on the back of the chauffeur's neck.)

My first call was to Mrs Lily Colefax, a rather bad-tempered widow of indeterminate years, who lives in a semi-detached cottage on the road leading to Ilfracombe.

It is, I think, quite fair to say that her husband Cyril had been something of a rogue. Technically, and as far as the boys and girls at the Inland Revenue were concerned, he earned his living as a bookie's runner. But the money he was paid for that particular obligation barely covered his costs of attending the seventy or eighty horse race meetings which he graced with his presence each year. His real income, not declared to the Inland Revenue for obvious reasons, was derived from lifting wallets, purses and watches. He was, in short, a professional pick pocket; a dip, a wallet lifter, a cutpurse.

Mr Colefax was extraordinarily keen on knitting and in the pursuit of this unusual hobby, he used to make seemingly endless supplies of scarves, woolly hats and jumpers. The vast majority of these invariably colourful and always well-made items were given to charity.

He once explained to me that he liked to knit in order to keep his fingers supple for his 'day job'.

Mr Colefax died of a massive heart attack while at the races in Exeter. That was about five years ago. The police took quite a while to identify him because they found seven wallets in his jacket and weren't sure whether he was Mr Pilkington of Plymouth, the Reverend Wilkins of Taunton, Mr Napton of Torrington, Mr Kennedy of Exmouth or Mr Jackson of Torquay. They were pretty sure that he wasn't Adebowale Akachi from the Serengeti or Mrs Pauline Twomely of Honiton.

Mrs Colefax is not clinically depressed but she is always miserable and if it is possible to find a pessimistic viewpoint to clasp to her bosom, she will assuredly find it and clutch it to her as tightly and as jealously as a little girl with a favourite doll or a dog with a much-loved bone.

Ever since I have known her, she has spent all her days looking backwards. However, instead of looking backwards and enjoying happy memories, she looks backwards and spends her days regretting all the bad things that have happened to her, the misfortunes which have troubled her, the rancour she has encountered, the mistakes other people have made (she has made very few, if any, of her own, of course), the disappointments she has endured and the frustrations she has faced.

I have always thought it something of a tactical error to spend your whole life looking backwards, over your shoulder. All you end up with is a sore neck. And, of course, you will never see the tree you bump into.

Mrs Colefax has, I suspect, always been a true pessimist; someone who has from childhood regarded life as a game which she was always destined to lose, and lose badly. There must have been occasional glimpses of hope, success, comfort and peace but these glimpses have to her always proved to be as illusory as heat haze mirages in the desert.

She spends a lot of time in bed, not because she needs to but because it enables her to gain the maximum amount of sympathy from relatives and neighbours (I think it would be stretching a point to include 'friends' in that list for I doubt if she has any) and because she is constantly rehearsing her dying moments and, indeed, her final words. She always speaks slowly and distinctly and once admitted to me that she did this so that if she died immediately, the witness would be able to tell the world what her final words had been. I have never been quite clear as to the purpose of this determination for I never heard her say anything which anyone could possibly regard as worthy of remembering and it doesn't seem likely that her last utterance would find its way into one of those strange little books of deathbed wisdom which appear on the bookshop shelves from time to time.

The one fun thing about her is that she fills her hot water bottle with whisky so that she can take generous nips throughout the day without anyone being any the wiser.

'Doesn't it make the whisky taste rubbery?' I asked her once.

'A little,' she admitted. 'But it's worth it not to have my neighbour nagging me about the perils of alcohol. Besides, regardless of the taste, it's still alcohol.'

'How much whisky do you put into the bottle?' I asked, assuming that she perhaps mixed the whisky half and half with water.

'The whisky is neat,' she said, with some pride.

Despite her faults, it is difficult not to admire and respect a woman who is prepared to put up with rubbery whisky for the sake of appearances.

'I'm going to die,' she announced, the moment I walked through her front door.

'It'll come to us all in the end,' I responded, cheerily.

'I'm going to die soon,' said Mrs Colefax.

'Why do you say that?'

'I'm 89-years-old, I have a weak heart and both my parents died when they were in their sixties.'

'You're not in bad condition,' I told her cheerily. 'With a bit of training you could be playing football for England next year.'

I know that it is never possible to make her smile but I always try.

She has been on the verge of death ever since I first came to Bilbury and I have for some time had a strong suspicion that she will outlive us all and that it will be my successor who eventually writes her death certificate when she finally meets her own dire expectations at the age of 153.

'I don't like football,' said Mrs Colefax, whose lack of a sense of humour is legendary.

I thought for a moment. 'Well, alternatively you could be dancing with the Royal Ballet company if you practise your arabesque and perfect your plie.'

'I don't like ballet.'

I gave up, as I usually do. 'What can I do for you today?' I asked.

'I have a pain just here,' she said, putting a hand on her right breast.

'In your breast?'

'Yes, if you must be so vulgar.'

'Breast isn't a vulgar word. It's an anatomical description of a part of the body.'

'It's rude. It's not a word which one would expect to hear in polite society.'

'I agree it's not a word one would bandy about if taking tea with the vicar's wife and the ladies of the Vicarage Sewing Circle,' I admitted, 'but I think its use is permissible in the sanctity of your own bedroom.'

'Hrmph!' said Mrs Colefax.

'Sit up, slip off your nightie and let me have a look.'

'I will do none of those things, young man!' said Mrs Colefax, defiantly. 'I'm not going to sit here looking at you while you're ogling my naked body.'

'I promise not to ogle. Close your eyes first. Then sit up, slip off your nightie and let me have a look.'

With obvious reluctance, Mrs Colefax closed her eyes, sat up and struggled out of her nightie.

'You'll have to remove your bra as well,' I told her.

She opened one eye and scowled at me.

'I need to look at the part that hurts.'

With even greater reluctance, and more of a struggle, Mrs Colefax succeeded in slipping her bra straps off her shoulders and pulling down her brassiere to release the contents.

'Do you always wear your bra in bed?'

'I certainly do,' she said. 'In case of emergencies.'

'What sort of emergencies?'

'In case of fire, for example.'

'How is your bra going to protect you against fire?'

'It will protect my modesty. If the house catches fire and a fireman climbs up a ladder to rescue me I don't want to be making an exhibition of myself.'

'You've got your nightie.'

'Young man, a woman with my attributes requires more support and protection than can be provided by a piece of unstructured flannel!'

I could see what she meant. Her breasts, milky white and decorated like a map with a network of blue veins, were voluminous.

'And then there are the burglars.'

I frowned. 'Burglars?'

'I don't want to be without my bra if burglars force their way into my bedroom.'

'No, I can see that,' I agreed. 'Where's the pain?'

'Just at the side here,' she said, rubbing the outer side of her left breast. 'But I have to confess that it seems to have eased a little.' She seemed puzzled, even saddened by this.

I leant forwards, and very gently plucked a small leather purse from inside her bra. There was a red mark on her skin where the purse, compressed by her bra, had pressed into the soft tissue of her breast. I showed the purse to her.

'Oh, good heavens!' she said. 'I usually keep that in the front of my bra, in what I think they call the cleavage area. It must have slipped round in the night.' Her cleavage would have provided enough storage space for the Bank of England to keep the nation's gold reserves safely hidden.

'And the pain has definitely eased?'

'Oh yes,' she said. 'I feel better now.'

I put the purse down on the bed beside her, told Mrs Colefax she could put her bra back into a more useful position and left as she struggled to re-confine her magnificent and generously proportioned superstructure.

My second visit had been requested by Frank, the landlord at our local public house, the Duck and Puddle. A year or so earlier Frank had a stroke and very nearly died. However, he made an excellent recovery. Under the careful and eagle eyed supervision of Gilly, his wife, he lost weight and learned to deal with stress more effectively. As a result, his blood pressure, which had previously been quite horrifyingly high, had come right down to levels approaching normality. I was very pleased with Frank's recovery and the progress he had made.

Frank usually visited me at the surgery but when he rang that morning, he had apologised and asked if I would call in at the Duck and Puddle to visit a customer who was staying in one of the rooms they rent out to visitors.

When I arrived I let myself in, since the front door was open, and found Frank and Gilly in the kitchen. They were having what some might call a blazing row but what they would call a slight disagreement about the way their dishwasher should be stacked.

The dishwasher was a brand new addition to the equipment at the public house and was widely believed to be the first in the village. No one else I knew had a dishwasher.

'The cups should all be up here,' insisted Frank, pointing to a portion of racking on the top level of the machine.

'That's silly!' said Gilly. 'It makes far more sense to put them down here.'

This looked likely to turn into one of those domestic discussions which have no end. 'I hate to interrupt and I hate to be a bore,' I said, 'but is there a chance you could discuss the planning procedures for the dishwasher when I've gone?'

I didn't particularly mind listening to their discussion, which promised to be quite entertaining, but I was keen to finish my calls and get the farrier before the sole of my shoe fell off completely.

They both apologised.

The Duck and Puddle has a couple of bedrooms which are let from time to time to tourists and others whose business brings them to Bilbury. I had stayed in one of the bedrooms myself when I had first arrived in the village. Indeed, I had, I remembered, been fortunate enough to occupy the only bedroom with its own bathroom.

As I followed Frank up the ancient, narrow staircase, I couldn't help remembering the day when, as a young, innocent and freshly qualified doctor, I had come to Bilbury to take up my position as assistant to Dr Brownlow. Frank and Gilly had been Mr and Mrs Parsons to me then.

I could even remember my first breakfast in the pub.

Most important of all, it was at the Duck and Puddle that I had first met Patsy, my wife. She'd been working at the pub, helping

Gilly and Frank. Her father, Mr Kennet, had been poorly, I remembered, and she'd been so worried that she'd burnt my traditional English breakfast to a crisp.

The breakfasts at the Duck and Puddle were designed to satisfy the calorific requirements of men who spent their days doing hard physical labour rather than driving round the countryside listening to people's chests and examining their feet. I had put on a stone in weight while I'd been a resident at the Duck and Puddle. I still hadn't got rid of all of it.

'Our guest is on a three day walking holiday,' said Frank, plodding slowly up the stairs ahead of me. 'He's an old-fashioned gentleman. In his late fifties, I would say. Solitary but well-mannered. He gets a lot of wind but always apologises if there's a particularly noisy eruption.'

'Eructations, borborygmi and flatulence,' I said.

'Pardon?' said Frank.

'Technical terms for wind coming up, wandering around inside or going out through the back door.'

'Ah!' said Frank, with an understanding nod. 'I always think that apologising for wind noises is the sign of a gentleman,' he murmured confidentially.

'You always do have a better class of customer here,' I said drily.

'We certainly do,' said Frank, slightly out of breath. 'We don't get the sort of people who steal the coat hooks from the back of the lavatory cubicle doors. Do you know, I heard at the last meeting of the Licensed Victuallers' Association that there are pubs in Barnstaple and Exeter where people do that?'

'Do you actually have coat hooks on the doors of your lavatory cubicles?'

'Well, as you well know, we only have one lavatory,' admitted Frank. 'And it doesn't have any coat hooks, as it happens, but if it did then I'm confident that our customers wouldn't steal them.'

The Duck and Puddle is still quaint and undamaged by progress with plastic. In most of England, the only places still quaint are the ones which are too poor to afford to modernise and too far off the beaten track to be troubled by intrusive health and safety busy bodies. And thus it is with the Duck and Puddle.

'Right,' I said. 'I'm glad we've got that cleared up.'

I didn't feel the need to remind him that most of the male customers of the Duck and Puddle use the laurel bush outside the pub's back door as a distribution centre for their waste beer. The bush is growing at an impressive rate and always seems greener than any other laurel bush in Devon.

I also didn't think it polite to point out that the last time I'd looked, the solitary lavatory at the Duck and Puddle had been entirely bereft of a proper door. Those using the facility had to make do with an old blanket nailed to the lintel. It would be difficult to fix a coat hook to a blanket.

Frank stopped in the narrow corridor upstairs and paused outside the door to one of the bedrooms. It was not the room where I had spent my first days and weeks in Bilbury. He knocked on the door, waited until he'd heard the occupant call 'Come in', opened it, led the way into the room, and introduced me. He then left.

'Sorry to bother you, doctor,' said the room's occupant.

He was, as Frank had said, a man who looked to be in his late fifties or possibly early sixties. He was lying in bed, dressed in heliotrope pyjamas buttoned up to the throat, he was pale, he was sweating slightly and, to put it mildly, he did not look like a man who was about to set off to run a marathon. The good news was that he was breathing quite normally and his pulse, though a little fast, was otherwise quite normal for an overweight, unfit man who had probably over-indulged. His waistline had probably last been seen circa 1957 and had, since then, been on the missing list.

He was, he told me, the manager of a large store in Leamington Spa but he was not, as he had indicated to Frank, on a walking holiday.

He had, to be blunt about it, run away from a job which he did not enjoy and which he found enormously stressful, from a marriage which was no more than a partnership of cold convenience, from grown-up children who demanded nothing from him but money (and plenty of it) and from neighbours whose main purpose in life seemed to be to slam car doors, use noisy garden machinery and breed uncontrollable offspring.

The fiction that he was on a solitary walking holiday was something he had used as an excuse before he had left and it was one which he had sustained for no other reason than that it seemed an easy explanation for his presence in Bilbury and at the Duck and Puddle.

His name was Elmore Hardwicke and, contrary to impressions, he was just 48-years-old. As already indicated, he was what used to be described as well upholstered and would now probably merit a rating of 'plump'. The cruel would have classified him as 'obese'. He did not look like a man who has an active gym membership.

Since Mr Hardwicke had run away from his life, you might have thought that fate would have given the poor fellow a break; a chance to enjoy his few days of escape.

But, sadly, fate does not work that way.

Since he was on holiday, Mr Hardwicke had decided to indulge himself and for each of the three mornings that he had been a guest at the Duck and Puddle, he had enjoyed the traditional English breakfast which has always been a keynote meal at Bilbury's finest, oldest and only eating establishment.

'You had the bacon and egg?'

'Four rashers and two eggs.'

'And the sausages?'

'Three of them. Cooked to perfection.' He closed his eyes, enjoying the sausages for a second time.

'Tomatoes and beans?'

'Of course.'

'Fried bread?'

'Two slices.'

'And toast?'

'Three slices, each covered with a thick layer of butter and blessed with handmade thick cut orange marmalade.'

'To drink?'

'A large glass of orange juice and a pot of English tea.'

'What do you eat for breakfast when you are at home?'

'A cup of tea and a bowl of cereal.'

'Your choice?'

He shook his head. 'At my wife's insistence.' The cereal looks like the sort of stuff people use to insulate their lofts. I suspect it tastes much the same too. She says it is a healthy breakfast, designed to keep me regular and to supply 87% of my daily vitamin requirements.' He shuddered. 'I hate cereals.'

'So your breakfast here is not the sort of thing you would eat at home?'

He shook his head. There was much sadness in the shaking and in his eyes. 'I've overdone it a little, haven't I?'

'A little, perhaps,' I agreed. 'What happened?'

'I got this terrible pain about an hour and a half ago,' said Mr Hardwicke. 'I thought I was going to die.'

'How long did the pain last?'

'No more than five minutes. It faded off quite quickly. It's pretty well gone now. But it's left me a little shaken.' He smiled ruefully. 'Like toothache going when you get to the dentist's surgery.'

'Where was the pain?'

'Just here,' he said, rubbing just underneath his ribs on the right hand side of his body. He did so gently and cautiously.

'Then what happened? After the pain had gone?'

'I just lay here for a while. The pain had gone but I was worried it might come back. I thought I ought to see someone and when Mrs Parsons came in to collect my tray I asked her if there was a local doctor I could see. She said she'd ring and ask you to come and visit me.'

'Have you ever had anything like this before?'

He shook his head. 'A little indigestion,' he admitted. 'And I do suffer with wind. I get a lot of wind. But this wasn't the same sort of pain as I get when I have indigestion.'

'Have you seen anyone about it? Your GP?'

'No.'

'Do you take anything?'

He opened the top drawer of the bedside cabinet and took out a packet of a proprietary indigestion remedy. 'I eat quite a lot of these.'

I nodded, told him to lie down a little flatter and peeled back the bedclothes. I didn't really need to examine him. I knew what was wrong with him. I estimate that at least 50% of the people who stay at the Duck and Puddle develop exactly the same symptoms and have the same underlying problem. I felt his tummy, checked his blood pressure and looked to make sure I wasn't missing anything else.

'I suspect that you have gall stones,' I told him.

'Do I need to go into hospital?'

128

'Not at the moment. You need to rest. And I'm afraid you need to avoid fatty foods for a while.'

'No more of Mrs Parson's breakfasts?'

'Just the toast and the tea I'm afraid.'

He looked very downcast.

'You can have marmalade.'

'Oh good. They have splendid marmalade here. Did you know that Gilly makes her own marmalade?'

I said that I did indeed know this. I told him that many Bilburian women made their own marmalade, using just about every fruit available. Patsy makes a wonderful cherry marmalade. Her grandmother once told me that the original marmalade was made with quinces.

'It's a funny word, isn't it? Marmalade. I wonder where the devil the name comes from?'

'There's a wonderfully silly tale that Mary Queen of Scots would ask for a fruit concoction whenever she felt a trifle queasy. 'Marie malade' the courtiers would call it. Hence the word 'marmalade'. People have been making marmalade for centuries. In the 17th century, a sophisticated traveller would pack his lunch box with a packet of macaroons, a jar of quince marmalade and a bottle of wine.'

'Golly!' said Mr Hardwicke.

'My wife's mother and grandmother make a good deal of marmalade,' I told him. 'It's also claimed that the word 'marmalade' comes from the word melimelum, the honey apple. But I prefer the Mary Queen of Scots story. And there's no reason you shouldn't have some baked beans and tomatoes.'

'How about a boiled egg?'

'OK. But just one.'

He looked much cheerier. 'Is that pain going to come back?'

'Probably not. But if it does you must ask them to telephone for me straight away.'

'And you'll come?'

'Of course.'

'Can I get up?'

'Definitely. There's no need for you to stay in bed. A leisurely walk wouldn't do you any harm.'

'But avoid rich foods?'

'Avoid fatty foods,' I told him. 'And when you get back home you should definitely avoid any breakfast cereals which look like insulation material or soundproofing.'

He brightened up. 'Can I tell my wife that?'

'Definitely. You can tell your wife that I advised you against eating breakfast cereals of any variety.'

'Oh good,' he said. 'May I really? That's rather splendid news.' He hesitated. 'I don't suppose you could…' He made the writing gesture that diners use when indicating to waiters that they're ready for the bill.

'Of course,' I said. I fished a piece of notepaper out of my black bag, took out my pen and wrote a short note confirming that Mr Edward Hardwicke of Leamington Spa was not allowed to eat breakfast cereals of any kind. I folded the note, placed it inside an envelope which I took from the pub's writing desk, and handed it to him.

'Thank you!' said Mr Hardwicke. 'Do you think I need to stay here a little while? In order to complete my recovery?'

'I think that would be wise.'

Mr Hardwicke seemed pleased by this. 'When do you think I'll be fit to travel?'

'Not for a week at least,' I told him. His eyes lit up. 'Come and see me in a week's time.' I told him.

I took a pad of certificates out of my bag, wrote out a sick note and handed that to him. 'Post this to your employer,' I told him. Mr Hardwicke definitely seemed to me like a man who needed a week's rest. And Bilbury is the perfect rest cure for those who have been battered by life.

He looked much brighter and more cheerful than he'd been when I'd arrived. A country doctor on his morning rounds cannot ask for much more than that.

When I left the pub, Gilly and Frank had completed their negotiations over the stacking of the dishwasher and were discussing their new menu.

They have, for reasons which escape most of their customers, recently taken to renaming some of the food items they sell in the bar in the style of one of those pretentious Chelsea wine bars. They still have a few items named after regular customers but the other items on their menu have been upgraded.

And so, the Duck and Puddle no longer sells 'crisps' (with cheese or onion being the choices) but offers a choice of either 'sodium infused ultra-crispy amuse-bouche pommes de terre fabrique avec fromage' or 'sodium infused ultra-crispy amuse bouche pomme de terre fabrique avec oignon'. Bottles of cola are now listed as 'hand selected, carbonato avec beaucoup des bulles dans l'eau'.

The translations were all done by Adrienne, my sister-in-law, whose claim to mastery of the French language is based on the fact that she once spent three whole days in Paris on a school trip.

Gilly and Frank were trying to decide whether they should add 'pain avec confiture' to their menu.

'Just stick with 'jam sandwich',' I told them. 'Otherwise no one in Bilbury will ever order one because they'll worry that it's something containing snails or frogs' legs.'

The Duck and Puddle is, I suspect, the only eating establishment in England which serves jam sandwiches. And it is definitely none the worse for it. When made with crusty farmhouse bread, cut thick and covered with lashings of home-made plum or strawberry preserve, a jam sandwich can be just as much of an epicurean delight as anything requiring a clutch of quail's eggs or a sauce which has taken a team of four trained chefs six hours to prepare.

'You know how to take the ground from beneath someone's feet!' said Frank.

'And the wind out of their sails!' added Gilly.

'Not to mention the clichés out of their conversation,' I said, managing, for once in my life, to produce a moderately bon mot which didn't wait three days to arrive.

Mr Hardwicke did come to see me a week later and he was much better than he had been when I'd seen him at the Duck and Puddle. He told me that he was ready to go back to work.

'You seem a lot more cheerful than you were a week ago,' I said.

'Oh I am, I am, doctor!' He moved forward a few inches in his chair, as though what he was about to tell me was both confidential and important. 'I have booked my room at the Duck and Puddle for another week. I shall be returning in three months' time,' said Mr Hardwicke.

'Splendid!' I said. I knew that Frank and Gilly would be pleased. They like to have what people in the hospitality trade refer to as 'repeat business'. 'You'll be coming by yourself again?'

'Oh yes. My wife and I live very separate lives. She enjoys pottery and likes to go on courses in East Anglia, Yorkshire, Provence and places like that.'

I couldn't help wondering what East Anglia, Yorkshire and Provence had in common but it seemed an irrelevant quibble so I merely nodded wisely.

'I have decided that I can cope perfectly well with my life as it is, if I know that every three months I can escape to Bilbury, to the peace and quiet and sanctity of the Duck and Puddle.'

'I understand,' I said, for I did, though I hoped that Mr Hardwicke would not be too disturbed if his stay happened to coincide with one of the Duck and Puddle's rather raucous skittle evenings.

'In fact I have given Mr and Mrs Parsons a series of dates when I believe I shall be able to partake of their hospitality, and they have agreed to reserve the room for me for a total of twelve periods of one week over each of the next three years. Mrs Parsons was kind enough to say that they will think of it as 'my' room.'

'So you'll be coming to Bilbury every three months?' I said, doing the sums in my head and feeling quite proud of myself at having done so without my head exploding.

'Exactly, doctor!' said Mr Hardwicke. 'I believe I shall become a regular in the village.' He smiled, and looked very pleased with himself. 'Mr and Mrs Parsons have told me that I may call them Frank and Gilly.'

'That's wonderful,' I agreed.

I have rarely seen anyone quite so happy. Mr Hardwicke had given himself something to live for and he was a contented man.

But that was a week ahead.

My third and final visit of the day was to Mr Warburton.

Mr Jason Warburton and his family live outside Bilbury. Indeed, they live outside the usual area I cover. Their home is close to South Molton.

The Warburton family had been patients of Dr Brownlow for longer than even he had been able to remember. The old man, Jason's great granddad, the patriarch of the family, had an unusual hobby. He used to enjoy going to funerals. Most of the time he didn't know the person who had died or any of the mourners. But he did know all the undertakers and most of the local clergy. He used to check out upcoming funerals in the local newspapers and he'd usually go to three or four funerals a week. It was his strange version of train spotting. He was 96 when he had his own funeral. His son, Jason's grandfather, was 75 when his Dad died but he was still known to everyone as 'Young Mr Warburton'.

When the younger branch of the family moved away from Bilbury, Dr Brownlow had, as a favour to the parents, agreed to keep them on as patients even though they were rather outside his catchment area. The agreement was that whenever possible they would visit the house for a consultation, only asking for a home visit when one was really needed. I had seen the latest Mrs Warburton once or twice, and I'd seen both of their children but I had never seen the youngest Mr Warburton before. And today it was young Mr Warburton who needed medical attention.

'I'm sorry I couldn't drive to your surgery,' said Mr Warburton, who is a plumber by trade and who didn't sound in the slightest bit apologetic. 'But when I woke up this morning I couldn't open my eyes. The lids were stuck. My wife bathed them open but they're sticky and itchy and watery and I really can't see well enough to drive the van. My wife doesn't drive.'

'That's fine,' I told him. I looked at his eyes. Both were clearly infected.

'I had a busy day ahead of me,' he said, full of self-importance. 'I was booked to do some plumbing for that bloke who does the cooking on the television. Whatsisname. The one with the beard and the glass eye. He's ever so famous. His name is on the tip of my tongue...'

When he talked, his dentures bobbed about as though dancing on independent suspension and it was easy to see that in addition to being something of a cockalorum, he was at least five times older than his teeth.

I didn't have the faintest idea who he was talking about. My knowledge of television cooks is limited. I remember once seeing a determined woman called Fanny Craddock doing something energetic with a bowlful of dough but that's about the extent of my knowledge in this area.

'Do you know how your eyes got infected?' I asked him.

'Rubbing them with dirty fingers probably,' said Mr Warburton. 'The wife is always telling me off for rubbing my eyes. And my fingers get dirty in my job. Toilets and such like.'

'Ah,' I said, taking out my prescription pad. 'Do you prefer ointment or drops?'

'Which do you recommend?'

'It's personal preference really,' I said. 'Personally, I prefer the drops because I find the ointment just tends to stick the eyelids together again. But some people don't like putting drops into their eyes.'

'I'll have the drops then please doctor. I've done plumbing for a lot of other celebrities.'

I wrote out the prescription for eye drops that would deal with his conjunctivitis.

'I sorted out a dripping tap for a cousin of that David Bowie,' he said. 'And I put in a new sink for a man who used to live in the same town as the drummer for The Who when he was growing up. He said he knew him quite well.'

'Really,' I said. 'That's very impressive.'

'I did some central heating work for Vince Hitzinger,' he said. 'Nice fellow. He gave me a copy of his last but one album.'

'My word,' I said. I hadn't heard of Mr Hitzinger but I assumed he was probably a musician of some kind and my knowledge of popular music is as limited as my knowledge of celebrity chefs. We do have one major rock star celebrity living in Bilbury but although he tours and sells records all around the world, no one recognises him and very few people know his identity. On stage he is wild, unkempt and rather alarming. He wears a good deal of make-up and a very impressive amount of hair. Off stage, without the hair or the make-up, he is shy and remarkably inconspicuous. It is difficult to reconcile the two.

'I thought of calling myself 'Plumber to the Stars',' said Mr Warburton. 'Have it painted on the side of the van. What do you think of that?'

'Very good,' I said. I suddenly remembered that six months earlier I had asked Mr Warburton to come out to Bilbury Grange to deal with a ball cock which had stuck and had flooded the downstairs lavatory. Our usual plumber had been in Torremolinos on a month's holiday. Mr Warburton had refused to come to Bilbury

Grange on the grounds that Bilbury was too far for him to travel. 'But,' I added, 'I think most people would be happy if they just found a plumber prepared to come out and deal with their leak.'

My comment was wasted. Mr Warburton either didn't remember or didn't care. He just took the prescription from me. 'How do we get hold of the drops?' he asked.

'The chemist in South Molton will have the drops in stock,' I said.

'You wouldn't fetch them for me, I suppose? It would save the wife a journey.'

'Afraid not,' I said. 'I'm a little busy. And South Molton is rather outside my catchment area.'

'Oh,' said Mr Warburton, clearly disappointed. 'I suppose I'll have to get the wife to go in and get them.'

'Your wife does drive then?'

'Oh yes.' Mr Warburton either didn't remember that he had lied about his wife not driving. Or, perhaps, he just didn't care. 'But she's out today. Since I didn't need the van she's gone into Barnstaple to do some shopping. There's a sale on at one of the shoe shops. They advertised it in last week's newspaper.' He shrugged. 'Anyway, better for me to use your petrol than mine, eh?'

I was furious. Mr Warburton could have easily asked his wife to drive him in to the surgery but instead he'd made me drive all the way to South Molton just to write a prescription for some eye drops.

'You might feel more comfortable with a doctor closer to home,' I said. 'There are plenty of good doctors in the South Molton area.'

'Oh no, we'll stick with you, doctor,' said Mr Warburton. 'The wife trusts you and says you're quite good with the kiddies. Myself, I liked old Dr Brownlow, of course. He looked after me when I was a nipper and I got used to him.'

'Of course,' I said.

'While you're here, would you give me a prescription for something for my stomach? One of those anti acid things. I never know which one to buy at the chemists. And if you give me a couple of packets, your stuff will be cheaper won't it? Give me something not too chalky but with a nice pepperminty taste.'

'Do you get a lot of stomach trouble?'

'Oh no, only on Saturdays if I go out with the lads. We go and have a curry and half a dozen pints of lager.'

'And you get an upset stomach?'

'Yeah. Sometimes. Not always. Sometimes.'

'Maybe you should stay at home on Saturdays,' I suggested. 'Or drink less lager.'

The plumber looked at me as if I were mad.

'Come and see me in the surgery if the stomach problem gets any worse,' I told him as I headed to the car.

'Hope you don't mind my mentioning it,' called Mr Warburton, as I left. 'But you want to get those shoes sorted out. Your sole is flapping. It'll trip you up if you're not careful.'

I thanked him and absquatulated without further delay.

God sends trials and tribulations in many strange forms and today He had sent him in the form of Mr Warburton the Plumber to the Stars.

But, finally, I was free to make my visit to get my shoes repaired.

Mr Albert Ross, the farrier, has lived in Bilbury all his life. His father and grandfather were both farriers. I have little doubt that his great grandfather was probably a farrier too. Indeed, I have no doubt that some member of his family was hard at work in Bosworth putting shoes on stallions, mares, fillies, ponies, hacks, geldings, chargers and nags back in the days while Richard III was wandering around offering to exchange his kingdom for a (doubtless nicely shod) horse.

Bilbury has at least one other professional farrier but Albert Ross is, as far as I know, the only one prepared to do a little human shoe cobbling on the side.

I found him in his smithy hammering a shoe onto one of the hind legs of a large beast which was standing quite still and seemed not in the slightest bit perturbed by what was happening at the far end of his body. A bored looking woman stood by the horse's front end, holding its head and looking on. She was, I remembered, the wife of a local farmer. I knew I had seen her recently but for the life of me I couldn't remember why or for what. I know I ought to remember every patient's name, ailment and treatment but I see dozens of patients every week and occasionally I simply cannot remember whether the tall, balding man is Mr Merriweather with the dermatitis or Mr Berryham with the swollen testicles.

I wondered if I should ask her how things were going but decided against the idea. I have found that when I can't remember why I've seen someone it is better not to refer to the consultation in any sort of social situation.

'Sorry to bother you,' I said, when the farrier paused and looked up. I suddenly realised that he and I had never met. 'I'm the doctor,' I said, introducing myself. 'My wife is Patsy, she was Patsy Kennet before we married.'

'I know Patsy,' said the farrier. He had the biggest eyebrows I'd ever seen on a human being. They looked like those big furry caterpillars which one occasionally sees around the place.

'The sole has come off my shoe,' I said, 'I know it may seem a bit of a cheek, but Patsy said you'd be able to mend it for me.'

'Let me finish this and I'll see to you,' said the farrier. He did not have much of a bedside manner but then I don't suppose there's much call for a bedside manner in his line of his work.

I sat down on a tree stump and watched the farrier at work. It occurred to me that it probably wasn't such a daft idea to expect a farrier to mend a pair of shoes. After all, the basic requirements are much the same: a hammer and a pocket full of nails.

It took the farrier no more than five minutes to finish putting fresh shoes onto the horse. The woman who had been holding the horse's head, handed the farrier a couple of folded notes which he slipped into the pouch at the front of his leather apron and then led the horse over to where I was sitting.

'Excuse me, doctor,' she said.

Not sure what she was excusing herself for, but aware that she needed me to move I stood up.

She then put one foot onto the tree stump which I had been using as a seat and which clearly had a primary function as a mounting block, and leapt with surprising agility up into the saddle still fastened to her doubtless trusty steed. As she did so, her surprisingly large bottom, encased in a pair of very tight riding jodhpurs, reminded me that on our last encounter I had treated her for a rather ripe case of external haemorrhoids. The jodhpurs she was wearing on this occasion were so tight that I could have probably made the diagnosis without asking her to undress.

I was now grateful that I hadn't asked her if her problem was any better when we'd met a few moments earlier. Even farmers and their wives (who all tend to have a very high level of embarrassment where bodily parts and functions are concerned) have been known to show signs of incipient shyness where piles are concerned.

The woman settled her well-built rear into the saddle and rode off with much clattering of hooves.

'Stand just there and put your foot up here,' said the farrier, indicating his leather covered lap.

Startled and slightly puzzled, I looked at him.

'Didn't you say you wanted your shoes mended?'

'Yes, please,' I said. I undid my shoelace and started to slip off a shoe.

'Don't do that!' said the farrier, rather crossly. 'You need to keep your shoes on.'

I looked at him.

'And come over here. I can't mend them unless you put your foot up on my lap, can I?'

I continued to look at him. 'You want to mend my shoes while I'm still wearing them?'

'Of course I do,' said the exasperated farrier. 'How else am I going to mend them?'

Patchy, who claims to have moments of raw brilliance, once said, life is like a game of crazy golf.

And I suddenly realised that he's absolutely right.

You just never know when you're going to come across a little windmill with three doors or a magic tower with a helter skelter leading directly into a sunken bucket filled with water.

Or a farrier wanting to hammer nails into your shoes while you're still wearing them.

I approached, turned away from him, bent my knee and put my shoe clad foot onto his lap.

'Is this going to hurt?' I asked, nervously, hoping that he was aware that the human foot is rather different in configuration, and pain susceptibility, to that of the horse.

'Not if you keep still,' he said.

I turned my head, nearly falling over as I do so, and watched him pick up a box of small cobbler's tacks. I was grateful he was going to use those, rather than the longer nails he used to affix metal shoes to horses.

'Did you know that the patron saint of cobblers is St Crispin?' he asked.

I said that I did not know this but that I did know that the patron saint of colic is St Erasmus while the patron saint of coin collectors is St Eligius. I knew this because Patchy, my favourite source of irrelevant but fascinating information, had told me.

To my astonishment and delight, the farrier successfully repaired both of my brown brogues. And after I'd changed my shoes, and put on my black pair, he mended those in precisely the same way. He did a damned good job on all four shoes and charged me a fraction of the price I'd have paid at the cobbler's shop in Barnstaple. I couldn't help wondering how many other people in Devon had enjoyed the delight of having their shoes repaired by a man who shoes horses for a living.

'You might have told me that he'd want to mend my shoes while I was still wearing them,' I said to Patsy when I got home.

'Would you have gone if I had?'

'Not likely!'

'That's why I didn't tell you,' said Patsy.

Ignorance is sometimes by far the better part of valour.

'Well, it was a strange experience but I feel great,' I said. 'In fact, I'm rather proud of myself and since there's a point to point meeting at Blackmoor gate next week, I think I'll perhaps enter. I'll see if I can find a jockey.'

Patsy laughed. 'I'm going to make myself a cup of tea,' she said, 'I'll get a bucket of water and fill a nosebag for you.'

I sometimes feel that I'm not always given the respect which is due to an established member of an ancient and dignified profession.

It Isn't Over Until the Fat Lady Slims

It was Peter Marshall who heard about it first.

Peter knows everything that happens in Bilbury for the simple reason that unless they fancy a round trip of over 20 miles into Barnstaple and back, everyone who lives in the village visits his shop several times a week. If you want a loaf of bread, a pint of milk, a postage stamp, a pair of shoelaces, a light bulb or a packet of goldfish food you have no choice but to visit Peter's excellent emporium. You can get beer, whisky and excellent sandwiches at the Duck and Puddle and you can get spiritual salvation at the village church, but for everything else you need to go to see Peter Marshall.

'Have you heard what Archie Meads is planning?' Peter asked me one afternoon about two months ago. I had popped in to pick up a couple of torch batteries, a new broom handle, a pair of socks and a bottle of shampoo for Patsy.

(It is difficult to think of any item that cannot be obtained from Peter's shop and I have, in the past, deliberately tried to stump him by asking for items which I did not think he would stock. These attempts have always proved unsuccessful and, as a result, we now own, but never use, a xylophone, a faux ivory back scratcher, a wine making kit and a six inch high model of the Eiffel Tower in a snow globe. I no longer try to catch him out for I have learned that it is better, safer and less expensive, to assume that Peter stocks at least one of everything ever made.)

Archie Meads is a local farmer. He doesn't live in Bilbury itself but he owns several hundred acres of farmland and a number of his largest fields are within the village boundary so what he does sometimes has an impact on our lives.

Mr Meads (he is so pompous that I doubt if his wife dares to call him 'Archie') lives in Monaco where he resides in exile in order to avoid paying any tax. Mr Meads has, over the years, experimented with various ways of adding to the fortune which he originally made from buying, selling and renting out small properties in the North of England. He was exposed several times, both in the newspapers and on television, and acquired something of a reputation as a 'slum landlord'. I don't think anyone in the area regrets that he chooses to live in Monaco.

Four years ago Mr Meads turned one of his fields into a caravan site, built a loo and shower block and invited the owners of touring caravans to stay there. There was some opposition from locals who felt that the Bilbury infrastructure was not capable of coping with an influx of summer visitors. We had already had considerable experience of the problems which too many tourists can have on a small community. A clutch of local councillors, were, however, wildly enthusiastic (and insistent that their enthusiasm had nothing whatsoever to do with the holidays they had enjoyed at Mr Meads' villa in Marbella) and the caravan park had been approved.

Sadly for Mr Meads, but luckily for the rest of us, the venture was woefully unsuccessful.

There were two problems which had been overlooked.

First, the field was on such a slope that caravanners found that whatever they did they simply could not make their temporary homes level.

Second, the lanes around Bilbury are very narrow and winding and are simply not well-suited for wide vehicles such as caravans. On at least three separate occasions, caravans actually got stuck and had to be removed with the aid of a tractor. Two of the caravans were destroyed completely.

The whole commercial experiment was not helped when persons unknown took to lighting large and smelly bonfires at weekends. A number of old carpets and unwanted car and tractor tyres were burnt and the caravan site eventually acquired an unpleasant reputation and a very poor rating in the Caravan Touring Society's brochure of sites.

'What's he planning this time?' I asked Peter, warily. Like most people in the village I am not a fan of Mr Meads or his activities.

'He's organising a three day music festival!' said Peter.

'A what!' I exclaimed.

'A festival with musical entertainment,' explained Peter. 'Like that thing they had in Woodstock a couple of years back.'

'When is it going to be?'

'In a couple of months' time I think. I'm glad I heard about it. I'll need to put in extra orders for food and drink. What sort of things do you think will sell best?'

'I should stock up well with marijuana,' I told him. 'But I suspect you might be in competition with some on-the-spot dealers.'

Peter looked shocked. 'I don't think my wholesalers sell that,' he said. 'Do you think I should just buy in some extra cans of cola and a few hundred boxes of crisps?'

'You might do better with bottles of lager and a few thousand hot dogs,' I said.

'Do you think so?'

'I don't have the foggiest, Peter,' I said, with an exasperated sigh. 'I have no idea what sort of things the people who go to music festivals are likely to buy.'

To be honest, I was cross because I knew that a music festival in Bilbury would create chaos, block all the lanes and bring most of the unpleasant qualities of the 20th century into our unworldly village. Peter, as usual, was thinking only of the money he could make.

When I got back to Bilbury Grange and told Patsy what was being planned, she too was appalled. 'They'll bring dogs with them,' she said. 'And their dogs will run loose and attack my Dad's sheep. There's bound to be a lot of noise and that will keep the children awake. And there are bound to be loads of people needing medical help. You're going to be rushed off your feet.'

I knew she was right. But after a couple of telephone calls I also knew that there was nothing we could do to stop the Festival happening.

When I telephoned the local council offices, I was told that the Festival still had the council's whole-hearted support. I wondered how many councillors were looking forward to enjoying more free holidays in Mr Meads' Spanish villa.

After a couple of months of waiting, the Festival was finally held last weekend. And it was every bit as awful as we had all feared.

I first became aware that the allotted fields were being prepared for the Festival when a man in jeans and a dirty T-shirt knocked on the door at Bilbury Grange.

'Are you the local quack?' he demanded brusquely.

I said that I was indeed the Bilbury doctor.

'You're needed at the Festival site,' he said. 'One of the scaffolders has cut himself. You'll have to sew him up.'

'How badly is he cut?' I asked. 'Does he need to go to hospital?'

'No time for hospital,' said the man in the grubby T-shirt. 'He's needed here. I'm in charge of the work gang. I've only got six guys and we've got to erect a stage, two lighting posts and a refreshment tent by the day after tomorrow.'

I checked my bag, to make sure that it contained a suture kit and a plentiful supply of suitable bandages, and followed the man in the grubby T-shirt to the site of the Festival.

Mr Meads had, to save money, decided to hold the event in the field where he'd already built a lavatory and shower block. And to take advantage of the natural slope of the field he had decided that the stage would be built at the bottom of the field, ensuring that all the spectators would be sitting in a very rough sort of amphitheatre.

Mr Meads hadn't bothered to cut the grass in the field, which was nearly a foot long, and the three huge lorries which had brought the scaffolding and boards for the stage had clearly been having some difficulty finding traction on the grass. There were huge gouges in the field where the lorries had skidded, stuck and been extricated.

My patient, who said his name was Duane, was sitting on the back of one of the lorries. He had a badly cut forearm and there was blood on his trousers, on his shirt and on the lorry.

'I thought I'd let it bleed a bit to wash out any of the dirt,' he said with a grin.

'Always a good idea,' I agreed. A little blood can go a long way but I still reckoned he must have lost half a pint. 'But it isn't really necessary to allow quite so much blood to come out.'

'Oh, I'll soon make that up again,' said Duane. 'A few lagers tonight should see me right. Where's the nearest pub?'

I told him how to get to the Duck and Puddle and couldn't help thinking that Frank and Gilly would probably welcome the extra business. Council rates, insurance and maintenance bills mean that they struggle to keep the pub alive. At least someone in the village would benefit from Mr Meads' latest business venture.

For the rest of us, with the exception of Peter Marshall, of course, the Music Festival would doubtless turn out to be a huge nuisance.

We choose to live in Bilbury because we enjoy peace and quiet and because we want to avoid as much of the 20th century as we can.

I sewed up Duane's arm without too much difficulty but as I was about to drive away, I found myself facing a girl of about 20 and a man who looked considerably older. She was wearing a bikini top and a pair of cut-off jeans. She had tattoos of what looked like dragons on the visible parts of her chest. I didn't like to look too closely. He was wearing a pair of old suit trousers, a pink shirt and an embroidered waistcoat. He had tattoos over most of his face. His tattoos appeared to be of satanic symbols and gave him an alarming look. I don't think he would have come high up on anyone's list of suitable candidates to play Father Christmas at a seasonal party.

'You the doc?' demanded the man.

I confirmed his diagnosis.

'I've left my contraceptive pills at home,' said the girl. 'I need another pack of pills.'

'You'll have to come to the surgery,' I told her.

'Why?' demanded the man aggressively. He moved closer to me, as though attempting to intimidate me. 'Can't you just give her some pills?' He pointed to my black bag. 'Haven't you got some in there?'

'I don't carry contraceptive pills,' I told him.

'Why do I have to come to the surgery?' asked the girl.

'Because I need to examine you and check your blood pressure and I can't do either of those standing in a field,' I told her.

'Just give her a prescription,' said the man. He took a roll of money out of his back pocket and peeled off a £10 note. 'Here,' he said. 'We can pay.'

'There's no need for you to pay me,' I told him.

I turned back to the girl. 'But I'm afraid you'll have to come to the surgery so that I can examine you. Then, if there aren't any problems, I can give you a prescription.'

'Where do we cash a prescription round here?' demanded the man.

'You'll have to go into Barnstaple.'

'Where's that?'

'About ten miles from here. If you drive west you can't miss it.'

'She needs the pills today,' insisted the man.

I looked at my watch and shook my head. 'She can come to my surgery this evening but the chemists in Barnstaple won't be open until tomorrow morning.'

'Are you prepared to take responsibility if she gets pregnant?'

'I don't think that would be my fault,' I told him.

'I need something for crabs as well,' said the girl.

'I'll need to examine you before I can give you anything,' I told her. I made a mental note to take a vaginal swab.

'She needs something now,' said the man, now threateningly. 'We can't wait until tomorrow.'

'Having trouble, doc?'

I turned and saw the man who was in charge of the work gang. He and Duane had come over to see what was going on.

'This bastard won't give Trace the stuff she needs,' said the man in the embroidered waistcoat. He wasn't so aggressive now. Indeed, there was a whine in his voice.

Duane, the man whose arm I had stitched looked at me, obviously expecting me to give my side of the story.

'I need to examine her,' I explained. 'And she needs to come to the next surgery if she wants me to treat her. I'll treat her if she comes to see me but I'm not going to perform an intimate examination and take the blood pressure of a perfectly healthy patient while we are both standing in a field.'

'Sounds fair enough to me,' said the man in charge. He turned to the man with the tattooed face and the waistcoat. 'Do as the doc says.'

The man with the tattooed face started to say something then nodded and turned away. The girl went with him.

'Sorry about that, doc,' said the man in charge.

'Who are they?' I asked.

'Just parasites. He's a small time dealer and pimp. She works for him.'

'They're not with you?'

'Bloody hell, not likely. I wouldn't employ either of them to clear up dogshit. He turns up at most of the festivals. Bad penny. Always has a girl or two with him. They've got a small tent in the next field.'

'Thanks for your help,' I said. 'He looked as if he was about to get a bit nasty.'

'Don't you worry about him, doc. If you have any trouble with him or anyone else you find me. My name's Rob. I'll be here until we all bugger off on Monday. Thanks for sewing up Duane.'

I went home. The girl didn't turn up at Bilbury Grange and I never saw her or the drug dealer again.

But that was just the beginning of my involvement with the Bilbury Music Festival.

Over the next few days I saw a seemingly endless stream of people requiring medical attention.

Mr Meads had made no provision for first aid treatment and I was the only person for miles around who was able and willing (albeit with, it has to be said, steadily increasing reluctance) to provide treatment for the staff, the musicians, the festival-goers and everyone else in attendance.

Most of the people I saw simply needed treatment for cuts and bruises and for coughs and colds and sore throats. A dozen or more needed contraceptive pills. There were a few with serious chest infections and, inevitably, quite a number with food poisoning. Three of the people I saw had problems caused by illegal drugs and several were suffering from alcohol poisoning. I saw a dozen or more with indigestion and several with sexually transmitted diseases. One girl who had a venereal infection wanted me to do tests on the six men whom she thought might have caused her problem. One girl wanted to know if you could get pregnant if you did it standing up and two wanted to know if you could get pregnant on the day when you lost your virginity. A singer with one of the bands wanted treatment for a sore throat and an ear infection. A guitarist who fell off the stage broke his wrist and had to be taken half way to Barnstaple by tractor because no ambulance could get anywhere near the Festival site. He was transferred to the ambulance about three miles away. The same procedure had to be followed when one of the men who had helped put up the stage was hit on the side of the head by an errant Frisbee. I feared that he might have a middle meningeal bleed, a type of brain haemorrhage which can be fatal, and insisted that he too go to hospital. He went with great reluctance but three hours later I was telephoned by one of the doctors at the hospital who told me that my diagnosis had been accurate and that if the young man hadn't been admitted to hospital he would have certainly died.

146

I made a mental note to insist that if the Music Festival was repeated then the organisers would be required to provide their own medical and first aid service – complete with a helicopter capable of taking patients to hospital.

I spent nearly an hour with an eight-year-old girl who was hysterical when I first saw her. She lived with her parents in Chelsea in London and had never been to the country before. After a long conversation I discovered that she was terrified that she was going to be eaten by the huge dog which she was convinced was roaming the countryside. It turned out that she had seen a pile of horse droppings in the lane and, never having seen a horse, had assumed that the not inconsiderable steaming heap had been produced by a wild dog of some variety. Under the circumstances, I think I too would have been terrified. I managed to settle her by arranging for her to see, and feed a chopped up apple to, a local horse in its field.

I syringed enough wax to make a candle from the ears of a drummer who suddenly discovered, to his delight, that he wasn't deaf after all.

I could and should have claimed payments from the National Health Service for treating all these patients but there was no time to fill in the necessary forms and so at the end of a hard weekend I had received a grand total of £1.75 in cash, three signed T-shirts and tickets for a rock concert in Berlin. I donated the T-shirts and the tickets to a raffle organised to raise money for our cottage hospital. The T-shirts and the tickets raised the princely sum of £7.47 for the hospital funds.

Since the roads were blocked with traffic I could not even use my bicycle, let alone the car, and I spent most of my time walking between Bilbury Grange and the site of the Festival.

I don't think anyone, not even Peter Marshall, had realised that in addition to providing almost non-stop musical entertainment, Mr Meads had also arranged for a small fair to set up in a neighbouring field. I saw several of the fair professionals over the next day or two, but I can only remember one of the patients I saw.

And for me, the story of that patient made the whole miserable weekend worthwhile.

'I need something to help me put on weight,' said a woman whose real name was Prudence Gaitskill but whose stage name was 'Fat Gertie' and whose advertising posters claimed that she was the fattest woman in Europe. She was certainly overweight; so rotund that she had considerable difficulty in walking and before she sat down she carefully put two dining chairs side by side, explaining that she didn't think one chair would be enough to hold her weight. Even with two chairs to sit on, her bottom overflowed at the sides of the chairs.

'You want to put on weight?' I said, rather startled, and assuming that I had perhaps misheard.

'Lord Snooty says that if I go under 30 stones he'll fire me and get another fat lady.'

'Lord Snooty?'

'That's what we all call him. He's the boss of the fair. His real name is Bernie Carrington though for show business purposes he calls himself Sir Bernard Carrington.' She laughed. 'He's no more a 'sir' than I'm the fattest woman in Europe.' She sighed and looked down at her hands which were clasped in her lap. 'I know for a fact that there are two women in France who are fatter than me. And I've heard that there is a woman in Scotland who could give me five stone.'

'You're losing weight?'

She nodded.

'How much have you lost?'

She looked down at her hands, still clasped in her lap, and mumbled something.

'How much?' I asked her. It was clear that she was reluctant to tell me. 'I need to know. You can tell me; I promise not to tell anyone else.'

'Five stone,' she whispered. 'Maybe six. I have to pad myself out a bit. But it means I can't wear the bikini. Lord Snooty is really nasty about that. But if I wear the bikini I can't pad myself out so much.'

'You wear a bikini?'

'When I'm working, yes. I sit in a cage in a bikini. The kids poke me with sticks.'

'How much do you weigh at the moment?'

'Just under 27 stone. A friend who has a haulage business weighed me on his lorry scales.' She paused. 'Actually, that was two months ago. I think I weigh less than that now. Probably no more than 24 or 25 stone I would guess.'

'How old are you?'

'Twenty two last birthday.'

I looked at her questioningly.

She blushed. 'Thirty three.'

'How long have you been a fat lady in a fair?'

'Ten or eleven years now.'

'Have you always been overweight?'

'Yes. I was a fat kid. I was going to do all sorts of things but I kept putting on weight and people never took me seriously. When I left university, no one would give me a job so I ended up working in a Fair. A man saw me in the street and offered me a job because his former fat lady had died on him. She was sat in a cage and they didn't know she was dead until the show closed that evening. She just died sitting on her throne.'

'Throne?'

'It's a sort of big chair. It looks a bit like a throne. It's more comfortable than an ordinary chair. If you have to sit in a cage for hours at a time, you need a comfortable chair. I have a bit of a bladder problem so I catheterise myself and wear a urine bag.'

'What did you study at university?'

'English literature. I wanted to be a teacher. But who'd hire a teacher who weighed 30 stone?' She shrugged. 'No one,' she said, answering her own question. 'No one, that's the answer.'

It all seemed so tragic that I didn't know what to say.

'I thought for a while it might be a hormonal problem,' she said. 'I had all the tests done but they couldn't find anything wrong with me. In the end I realised the doctors were using me as a sort of freak show too. They kept inviting me to appear at conferences and sit on the stage at lecture halls. They paid my expenses but never paid me a fee. So in the end I gave up on the doctors.'

'How do you get about? How did you get here today?'

'A friend brought me. His name is William Pears. He's the dwarf. He's got a tattoo of a lion on his chest and a tattoo of Queen Victoria on his back. He does a bit of juggling and fire eating and sits in a chair while people pay five pence to throw wet sponges at him. I've got a little van with a lift at the back. I sit on this sort of sling thing and he hoists me into the back of the van. He drives. I can't drive because I couldn't fit in the driving seat and even if I could I wouldn't be able to get behind the steering wheel and press the pedals, would I?'

'Where's your friend now?'

'He's outside, sitting in the van. He'll wait for me.'

'And you want to put back all the weight you've lost?'

'And a bit extra if possible. There must be something you can give me.'

'Do you want to be a fat lady in a fair for ever?'

'No, of course I damned well don't!' she said, crossly. A tear appeared in the corner of one eye. 'Do you think I like sitting on a stupid throne, in an iron cage, and having kids poke me with sticks? Do you know Lord bloody Snooty rents out the sticks so that the kids can poke me? And you wouldn't believe where they do the poking. They're always trying to pull off my bikini top. The girls are the worst. You wouldn't think that, would you?'

'Do you have any idea why you might have lost so much weight?'

'I've lost my appetite a bit.'

'Do you have any pain?'

'More a discomfort. Not really a pain.'

'Whereabouts?'

'In my lower abdomen.'

'How are your bowels?'

She blushed.

'Any problems?'

'Some bleeding.'

'You lose blood rectally?'

She nodded.

'For how long?'

'A month. Maybe two months.'

'Much?'

She nodded. 'Quite a bit.'

'And how have your bowel movements been?'

'I'm sorry I lost my temper with you a bit earlier. When I said that about people poking me with sticks.'

'That's OK,' I said. 'Have you had any diarrhoea? Constipation?'

'The only thing is that when I've been to the toilet I always feel as if I haven't finished.' She was now blushing deep red through embarrassment.

I tried to help her. 'As though there's more that needs to come out?'

'Exactly. That's it.'

'But there isn't?'

'No, there isn't.'

'I need to examine you.'

'You could save us both a lot of bother and just give me a prescription for something to help me put on weight.'

'I need to examine you.'

She sighed.

'I really do need to examine you,' I said again.

She looked at me and then glanced at my examination couch but she didn't say anything.

I looked at her and spoke softly. 'You're not going to be able to get up onto the couch are you?'

'No.'

'Then you'll have to lie down on the floor and I'll examine you there.'

She thought about it for a moment or two and then nodded. 'OK,' she whispered.

It took half an hour to get her undressed and lying down on the floor. Patsy brought a fresh sheet and laid it down on the floor so that Miss Gaitskill didn't have to lie down on the carpet. And it was Patsy who helped her undress.

I'm sure that I am not the only person to have noticed that small, even trivial, seeming incidents in people's lives can sometimes lead directly to momentous, life changing consequences.

For example, a friend with whom I was at medical school suffered serious damage to his hearing when he was a boy. He was away on holiday at a resort in a relatively unpopulated part of North Africa with his parents when he developed mumps. The non-availability of doctors meant that the infection wasn't properly treated and, as a result, he developed a type of deafness which steadily got worse as he got older. When he qualified as a doctor, my pal realised that he was never going to be able to take a job working with patients directly. His worsening deafness made it impossible for him to talk easily to patients or colleagues. And so he deliberately chose to become a radiologist. He could sit in silence studying X-rays and didn't need to talk to anyone. Everyone who worked with him claimed that he was the best damned radiologist they'd ever come across. My pal claimed that if he was good at reading X-rays it was because of, rather than in spite of, his deafness. Because people tended not to talk to him about the patients whose X-rays he was studying, he could look at the pictures without any preconceived ideas.

But the fact is that he almost certainly only became a radiologist because he'd been on holiday, caught mumps and not been properly treated. His whole life was changed by his parents' choice of a holiday destination.

I think Miss Wakefield would agree with me that her visit to my surgery for help in putting on weight was one of those apparently minor incidents which eventually lead to life changing consequences.

As I had feared, I couldn't find anything when I examined her abdomen. She was so obese that there could have been a football hiding inside her and I wouldn't have been able to feel it. But I found out what was wrong with Miss Gaitskill when I finally managed to turn her on her side so that I could examine her rectum.

As I had feared and expected, she had cancer. The only good news was that I could find no sign that the cancer had spread into her lymph nodes.

When I had finished examining her and had cleaned up the blood which had come from her back passage, I helped her dress and sit back on the two chairs.

'It's cancer, isn't it?' she said.

'I think it is,' I agreed.

She sighed. It was a sigh of weariness, rather than sadness. The sigh of a woman who has been fighting life for so long that she no longer feels anything very much.

'I'm going to fix up for you to see someone at the hospital tomorrow,' I told her.

'Tomorrow? So quickly?'

'Tomorrow,' I insisted. 'If you leave North Devon and go somewhere else you will probably never get this sorted.'

'Is it something that can be sorted?'

'Yes, I think so.'

'Lord Snooty will have a fit.'

'Do you care?'

She smiled. 'Not really.'

I helped her up off the chairs and told her to get herself to the hospital by 9 a.m. the following morning. 'You may have to wait to be seen,' I told her. 'But I will fix you an appointment with one of the surgeons.'

She promised that she would do as I had asked.

And she did.

The surgeon confirmed my, and her, suspicions. He said that he would not normally have operated on anyone so vastly overweight but in view of the position of the tumour he thought he could reach it without waiting for her to lose weight. He said he wanted to operate quickly before the cancer spread.

The operation was a success.

Miss Gaitskill left the hospital two weeks later and came back to see me.

'I'm going to try to lose weight,' she said. 'I want to go into hospital where I can have help controlling what I eat. While I was in hospital in Barnstaple I heard a lot about your hospital here in Bilbury. I have some savings and I want you to let me stay there. I'll pay the same as I would have to pay a private hospital and you can use the money to help keep your hospital going.'

I told her I would have to think about it. I explained that she had to come back to see me the next day after I had spoken to Bradshaw, my practice nurse. Bradsaw, a genial octogenarian, also runs the Brownlow Country Hotel where he is officially the manager.

(I explained to Miss Gaitskill that our local cottage hospital is so named to avoid administrative complications with NHS bureaucrats. I also explained that although the hospital is called a hotel it is run efficiently and effectively by Bradshaw, who is in every practical sense the matron, together with his team of local volunteers.)

Miss Gaitskill stayed the night at the Duck and Puddle and when my surgery opened the following morning, she was standing on the doorstep.

I told her that we would initially take her for a month at the hospital and that she could stay there for as long as she continued to lose weight unless there was some sort of dire emergency and we needed her bed in which case we would expect her to move into the Duck and Puddle. I told her that I expected her to lose a quarter of a stone a week for the first month and, therefore, a stone in the first month. And I told her that she had to obey Bradshaw's every instruction and, indeed, his every whim relating to her diet. She accepted these rules without protest.

William Pears, the dwarf, who had given up the Fair to stay with her, took a room at the Duck and Puddle and a job as a counter assistant in a shop in Combe Martin. He stood on a box behind the counter and was popular with everyone. It was, he said, the most dignified work he had ever done. It was the first time he'd been treated as a human being rather than as a freak.

Miss Gaitskill lost a stone in the first fortnight and a stone and a half in the first month. After three months she weighed under 20 stone and I could weigh her on the scales in my consulting room. It was the first time she could remember being able to weigh herself on ordinary household weighing scales. She stayed on at our hospital for six months and while she was there she applied for a place at a teacher training college. She was successful and she eventually trained as a teacher of English language and English literature.

Half way through her training, Miss Gaitskill became Mrs Pears and the couple got married in Bilbury. She weighed just over 11 stone at the time and Patsy and I, who were invited to the wedding, cried almost all the way through. They made a lovely couple.

Every Christmas, Patsy and I receive a card and a long, hand-written letter from them. And every summer they visit Bilbury and stay in the Duck and Puddle for a week.

'I have travelled around the country a good deal,' she once told me, 'and there are desolate parts of Devon and Cornwall where newcomers are regarded as strangers unless their families have lived there for three or four generations. Bilbury is different in that the welcome it gives to newcomers reminds me more of one of those inner city areas in the English Midlands where life is harsh but the people are invariably kind and welcoming to strangers.'

Her words have stayed with me for they were, I think, honest and well earned. Everyone I've ever spoken to, says that Bilbury is, for those who choose to live there, the most welcoming place they've ever visited.

As far as the villagers were concerned, the Bilbury Music Festival (and the Fair which accompanied it) was a total disaster.

The lanes were clogged with traffic and no one could sleep for three nights because of the noise. Peter Marshall sold less food and drink than usual because the folk attending the Festival either brought their food with them or bought everything they needed at the stall on site. And the residents of Bilbury, who were marooned in their homes and unable to reach the shop because of the traffic jams, couldn't buy anything either. The Duck and Puddle sold some beer to the men putting up the scaffolding but none of the Festival goers visited the pub, and the scaffold erectors were such a fearsome looking bunch that the pub regulars stayed at home; locking their doors, drawing their curtains and existing on whatever food and drink they could find at the back of their larders.

The only good news was that the event proved to be a financial failure too.

The cost of paying the bands, the stage erectors and the other assorted folk required to organise the event was far greater than the money raised from ticket sales and from the sale of food and drink. Many of those who came to the Festival did not bother to buy tickets, realising that if they camped in nearby fields they could see and hear what was happening almost as well as if they were in the field where the event was being held.

And so, it was with considerable relief that the villagers heard that Mr Meads would not be holding another festival.

Paula Temple

'What evidence is there for your claim?' I asked.

I thought for a moment.

'The available evidence in support of my argument goes back a decade to the early part of the 1960s,' I replied.

'But a good many people have been helped by these drugs,' I argued.

'On the surface that appears to be true,' I agreed. 'But will that still be true in the long term?'

'There are some who would say that you are simply scaremongering.'

'That's unfair. I'm merely trying to draw attention to a very real problem.'

I have always tried to keep the talking to myself internalised, or at the very least sotto voce, but on this occasion I seemed to have spoken out loudly enough for other people to hear.

I was practising for a meeting that I was due to attend later that evening.

I was pretty sure that I was going to be given a rough time and I wanted to try to prepare myself.

I couldn't help noticing that a couple of visitors who were sitting in a far corner of the pub were looking across at me. They had clearly overheard the two halves of my conversation, and realising that there was no party of the second party, were, to say the very least, a trifle perturbed. To be honest, I couldn't blame them. I always tend to look with suspicion on individuals who have lengthy discussions with themselves.

The male half of the couple called over Frank.

'Who's that?' I heard him ask. He made no attempt to lower his voice.

'Does he need a doctor?' asked the female half of the couple.

'Oh, that is the doctor,' said Frank cheerily. 'Can I get you another drink?'

'Just the bill, please,' said the man, standing up. He looked across at me, rather nervously.

I heard the woman say something to Frank but couldn't make out what it was. The man paid and they left.

'What did that woman say to you?' I asked Frank, who was picking up their empty glasses.

Frank grinned and walked across to where I was sitting. 'She said she was glad they don't live here and have you as their doctor,' he said. He looked down at my empty coffee cup. 'Do you want a refill?'

I looked at my watch and sighed. 'I'd better be going,' I said.

I had stopped in at the Duck and Puddle on my way to a meeting of our local medical society. The meeting was being held in a hotel halfway to Exeter. I had been persuaded to give a talk about the dangers of a group of drugs known as benzodiazepines – the best known of which were a number of enormously successful products with names such as Valium, Librium and Ativan.

The main problem I faced was that almost all other members of the medical profession were uncritically enthusiastic about benzodiazepines. The drugs were rapidly becoming the world's most popular medicines.

The Valium story began in the 1930s when a Dr Leo H Sternbach was working as a research assistant at the University of Krakow in Poland. He was investigating the benzophenones and heptoxdiazines. Little happened until 1954, when Dr Sternbach was working in the New Jersey laboratories of a company called Hoffman La Roche. The result of his last experiment was called Ro5-0690 and was initially shelved as being of little interest.

However, a couple of years later, in 1957, Ro5-0690 was submitted for testing by Roche's Director of Pharmacological Research and a report was published showing that the drug was a hypnotic, a sedative and a muscle relaxant. It was a new chemical substance and the company thought it rather promising. In late 1958, Roche did more tests on the drug and found that it was effective at treating anxiety and tension. The drug was called chlordiazepoxide. The next step was that on February 24th 1960, the American Food and Drug Administration approved the drug for human use. A few weeks later, the drug was launched under the brand name of Librium.

Before the end of 1960 other drug companies, Include Wyeth Laboratories had introduced benzodiazepines of their own. In no time at all, GPs and other doctors were prescribing these drugs for an enormous range of physical and mental problems. It is difficult to think of a medical condition for which benzodiazepines were not prescribed. If you went to see a GP in 1970, you had a better than one in twenty chance that you would come away with a prescription for a benzodiazepine. A little later, one in five people who was given a prescription was given a prescription for one of these drugs.

However, I was not a fan of benzodiazepines.

What worried me was the fact that even in those early days there was evidence that these drugs might cause problems.

In 1961, a clinical report appeared in the journal *Psyschopharmacologia* which warned that patients were becoming addicted to chlordiazepoxide. In 1968, a paper in the *Journal of the American Medical Association* showed that benzodiazepines caused depression and suicidal thoughts. Then in 1970, in a book called *Discoveries in Biological Psychiatry*, edited by Ayd and Blackell, Frank Ayd wrote: 'Although vast quantities of minor tranquillisers have been prescribed, it must be stated that not all have been dispensed judiciously by some practitioners. Such misuse is indicative of physicians who unwisely accede to the demands of patients or who supplant sound clinical judgement or expediency'.

And in 1972, the *American Journal of Psychiatry* published a paper describing how patients on diazepam (the generic name for Valium) had exhibited symptoms which included apprehension, insomnia and depression. The patients had previously been emotionally stable. When the patients were taken off the drugs, their symptoms disappeared.

During the early 1970s, I had written a number of articles about the dangers of benzodiazepines. My articles, written from my little country practice, had caused something of a stir and I was rapidly becoming a 'hate' figure among doctors all over the country.

History is full of examples of original thinkers who have been scorned, laughed at, ruined and imprisoned for daring to be creative and original and (most heinous a crime of all) for having the temerity to question (and therefore threaten) the status and authority of the establishment.

Socrates was condemned to death for being too curious. Dante was condemned to be burned at the stake. The works of Confucius were still banned in China two and a half thousand years after his death. Spinoza was denounced for being independent and every schoolchild knows about Galileo's battles with the Church. Aureolus Philippus Theophrastus Bombastus von Hohenheim (better known to his chums as Paracelsus) was the greatest influence on medical thinking since Hippocrates but the establishment regarded him as a dangerous trouble maker and persecuted him all around Europe. (He is still regarded with considerable fear and distaste by the medical establishment which, on the whole, prefers not to acknowledge his existence or his importance.)

Ignaz Semmelweiss, the Austrian obstetrician, was ostracised by the medical profession for daring to criticise filthy medical practices. He was ridiculed for his views on puerperal fever, and so depressed by the opposition from the medical establishment that he became insane.

The incomparable Henry David Thoreau was imprisoned for sticking to his ideals. Wilbur and Orville Wright were dismissed as hoaxers by the US Army and most American scientists. When Wilhelm Rontgen discovered X-rays, his achievement was described as an elaborate hoax by one of Britain's most eminent scientists. Michael Servetus, the Spanish physician who discovered the circulation of the blood to and from the lungs, was executed.

The relationship between a diet low in vitamin C and the development of scurvy was first described in 1636 by John Woodall. James Lind reintroduced the idea in 1747 but it wasn't until 1795 that the British Admiralty decreed that that lemon juice should be part of every sailor's diet. Only God can possibly know how many sailors died as a result of this appalling example of cooperative prejudice.

And then there was Dr John Snow.

In the years 1848 and 1859, cholera killed thousands of people in London. Snow decided that people were contracting the disease from their drinking water and argued that the solution was to keep the sewage away from the drinking water supplies. Because the commonest symptoms, diarrhoea and vomiting, both involved the alimentary tract, he decided that the disease must be transmitted by something which had been ingested rather than something carried in the air.

In 1849, when a fresh cholera outbreak hit London, Snow gave up his general practice in order to investigate his theory. His first conclusive proof came from a survey of the district around Golden Square in the centre of London. At that time, piped water was not supplied to all houses in the area, and most people took their water from pumps and wells. A pump in Broad Street supplied the majority of the local inhabitants, and Snow's enquiries persuaded him that a cholera epidemic in the area was directly linked to the use of that particular pump. (A later investigation showed that the brick lining of a cesspool about three feet away from the well was cracked and that the leaky cesspool was contaminating the drinking water.) To prevent the further spread of the cholera, Snow had the pump's handle removed so that water could no longer be drawn from the contaminated water. Snow was not exactly the flavour of the month among his colleagues.

The original inventors of turbine power, the electric telegraph, the electric light, television and space travel were all laughed at or ignored by the scientific establishment. William Reich's books were considered so dangerous that they were burned by the Nazis in Germany in the 1930s and by the Federal Food and Drug Administration in the United States in the 1960s.

My own campaign (for that was what it had become) was a comparatively modest one. But it was, nevertheless, quite real and to me it seemed important.

The problem, of course, was that even in the 1970s, all parts of the establishment were pretty well stocked with men and women who had an aversion to anything which threatened the status quo – and which were, in particular, a threat to the medical profession's very close and undeniably self-serving relationship with the pharmaceutical industry.

And the medical establishment was (and to a large extent still is) particularly hide bound and especially reluctant to accept new theories or challenges to the accepted 'norm'.

The rather sad truth is that I was discovering that keeping an open mind, and being prepared to question existing ways of doing things, are not likely to do a young doctor's career much good at all. When I once commented on a radio programme that it was important to keep an open mind about new developments, one of the other guests, a very eminent member of the medical establishment, snorted and then remarked, in a rather contemptuous tone, that in his view, open minds were empty minds.

My interest in benzodiazepines had been aroused when a patient called Paula Temple had moved to Bilbury.

Miss Temple had come to Bilbury from Finchley, a suburb in North London. She had spent most of her life working in a pharmacy and had never been married. She had been engaged in 1939 but her fiancé, who had been a navigator on a Royal Air Force bomber, had died during a raid on Germany during World War II. Miss Temple and her fiancé had been due to marry the week after he had died and, like many women in similar circumstances, she had remained steadfastly loyal to his memory.

When I asked Miss Temple why she had chosen to retire to Bilbury she told me that, although she hadn't been to North Devon for over a half a century, she had spent many happy childhood holidays in a cottage in Bilbury. Her parents, clearly creatures of habit, had rented the cottage for two weeks every summer. Miss Temple decided that since the happiest days of the first part of her life had been spent in Bilbury, she might like to spend the final part of her life in the same place – in the hope that she might be able to rediscover some of the sense of peace and happiness she had enjoyed as a young girl.

She told me that when she had spent a few days in North Devon looking at cottages in and around the village, she had been struck by the fact that very little had changed while she had been elsewhere.

'The cars look different, and there are far more of them, and fashions have changed,' she said, 'but apart from that there really doesn't seem to have been much change. London and other cities have changed enormously in the last half a century. But Bilbury has remained as I remembered it.'

Two years before retiring, and choosing to move to Bilbury, Miss Temple's mother had died.

It had been a difficult time for the younger woman.

Mrs Temple had died of cancer and had required a good deal of nursing. In the last year and a half of her life she had also developed some form of dementia.

161

Looking after her aged mother had, for Miss Temple, been an exhausting experience in every way. It had been physically exhausting. It had been mentally exhausting. And it had been emotionally exhausting.

In a doubtless well-meaning attempt to help Miss Temple cope with the task of looking after her mother, while holding down a full-time job in order to pay the bills, the family doctor had prescribed Librium capsules.

And Miss Temple had been taking the drug for over four years. When I first met her she had come to the surgery to request another prescription for her Librium. She was quite insistent that I should give her the drugs.

'After my mother died I decided that I wanted to try without the pills,' said Miss Temple. 'So, foolishly, I just stopped taking them. As a result I became very ill.'

I asked her what symptoms she had noticed when she'd tried giving up the capsules.

'I started to shake, I was dizzy, I couldn't rest or relax or sleep,' she told me. 'I couldn't concentrate, I started to suffer from nausea and headaches and I felt very depressed. When I told my doctor about my symptoms, he said they showed that I needed to keep taking the capsules. So I started taking them again and the worst of my symptoms disappeared within a day or two. So I thought the doctor was probably right and that I should just keep on with the capsules as he advised.'

'What made you feel that you should stop taking the Librium?' I asked her.

'I felt that the drug was making me feel numb and fuzzy,' she said. 'I realised that I was sort of sleep walking through life, not properly aware of everything about me. It was as though I was seeing life through a thick veil of cotton wool.'

'But when you stopped them you became more anxious?'

'I felt terribly anxious; as though I were going to die.'

'And how do you feel now that you're taking them again?'

'I feel calmer than I did when I tried to stop them. But I still feel fuzzy and slow. I feel as though I'm drugged – as though I'd been anaesthetised ready for an operation but the anaesthetic hadn't properly taken effect. I feel like that all the time.'

I didn't know much about benzodiazepines at the time.

I had never prescribed them for my patients because I had felt unhappy about them.

But it was pretty obvious that Miss Temple was addicted to the drug she was taking and that if she was going to stop taking it then she would have to withdraw slowly over a period of weeks, possibly even months, rather than immediately or even over a period of days. I told her this and she asked me if I would help her through the withdrawal process.

And for the next three months I helped her cut down her daily dosage of Librium.

I read a few books and research articles on the subject and decided that it would be sensible to halve her dose every two weeks or so. To make things easier I switched her from Librium to Valium (an expert in drug addiction problems whom I consulted seemed to think that the products were pretty well interchangeable) because Valium was available in smaller dose tablets – and the low dose tablets could be cut in half with a knife in order to lower the dose even more.

The addiction expert to whom I spoke reminded me that what was happening with benzodiazepines had happened twice before. In the 1950s, huge numbers of patients were addicted to barbiturates which had been wildly over-prescribed as panacea drugs by enthusiastic doctors. And in the early part of the 20th century, there were similar problems with widespread addiction to potassium bromide. Once again these drugs had been over-prescribed by doctors.

I also talked to my friend Will, who is a GP in the English Midlands.

He has a steady turnover of patients, since people move in and out of his practice area far faster than they do in Bilbury, and he had seen many patients hooked on large doses of Valium, Librium, Ativan and other brands of benzodiazepine.

Will told me that he considered that benzodiazepine addiction was going to be a huge problem in the future – largely because so many doctors still didn't recognise that the drugs were addictive. Sadly, he felt that other doctors didn't recognise the size of the impending problem. His partners were still happily doling out benzodiazepines to a high proportion of their patients and using them to treat every disease imaginable – and certainly everything for which there wasn't already a specific drug.

Gradually, Miss Temple re-discovered her old self.

It was a difficult few months but eventually she told me that everything in the world seemed to be improving: she enjoyed music more, the colours around her seemed brighter and she enjoyed reading books again.

It was a very slow process and there were some very bad days. It seemed to me that the drug had suppressed the feelings that she'd had when her mother was ill and that as she came off the drug those old, hidden feelings all came out from where they'd been temporarily packed away. There were days when she cried and nights when she couldn't sleep. She went through the mourning process which had been numbed by the Librium she had been taking and she had to endure again the anguish of her mother's prolonged illness.

'I'm sure my doctor in London thought he was helping me,' said Miss Temple. 'He was a kind man. But I think he just accepted what the drug company told him. I wish he had just allowed me to deal with the feelings I had at the time I had them. Numbing me with the pills has just delayed things and it is now much harder to deal with those hidden emotions.'

But she did succeed in 'kicking' her prescription drug addiction. It took slightly more than three months but after that time she was a different woman. She looked brighter and more alert. She took a much more active interest in the world around her.

It was my experience with Miss Temple which had inspired me to do so much research into benzodiazepine drugs. And, although I did not mention her name, of course, she was the patient whose problems I described when I gave my lecture.

Sadly, the audience's response was not good.

Most of the doctors who were present at the meeting were enthusiastic prescribers of drugs such as Valium and Librium and they found that their patients welcomed them.

'I don't think I could run my practice without these drugs,' said one GP. 'I find them the most useful multi-purpose drug available. Vast numbers of my patients take them without any noticeable side effects.'

'But have they tried stopping the drugs?' I asked.

'Why on earth would they want to stop the drugs?' he demanded. 'They like the drugs. They need them. They don't want to give them up.'

Another GP told me that he believed that I should be struck off the medical register for even suggesting that the drugs should be controlled.

And so it went on.

Every doctor who spoke attacked my views. No one agreed with me that benzodiazepines were, or ever could be, any sort of problem.

Eventually, as my colleagues sipped their coffees, nibbled their biscuits and pocketed the free gifts which they'd been given by the drug company representatives who are always present whenever three or more doctors meet, I slipped away, climbed into the old Rolls and drove back to Bilbury.

I remember being angry, frustrated and keen to get away from the damned place.

Spreading the word about benzodiazepines was clearly going to take a long time, and be a hard battle. But it was, I felt, a battle that had to be fought.

'How did it go?' asked Patsy, when I arrived back at Bilbury Grange.

She had offered to accompany me to the lecture but I'd had a feeling that things would not go well and I'd advised her to stay at home. She always gets upset when she sees or hears me being attacked. Besides, someone always has to be at the house to answer the telephone and Miss Johnson, who usually comes in to take messages and babysit the children, was away at her sister's home for a short holiday.

I didn't say anything in response to Patsy's question but simply put my arms around her and held her tight.

'Bad?

'Pretty bad.'

'Do you want to talk about it?'

'Later. Much later. Tomorrow, maybe.'

'I've got a hot apple pie in the oven.'

'Custard?'

'Take me five minutes.'

Comfort food.

While Patsy prepared the custard for the apple pie I put on my old, comfortable slippers, poured myself a malt whisky, sat down in my favourite chair in front of the log fire and welcomed Ben, my elderly but ever-faithful dog, up onto my lap.

The cats were curled up on the rug in front of the fire.

The logs in the fireplace were from an old apple tree which had been cut down in our orchard the year before. Apple wood smells sweet when it burns.

I picked up a copy of our local parish newsletter, which is always a joy, and looked through the small advertisements at the back. Mrs Younger was advertising her sock darning service. Mr Pershore was advertising his tractor for sale. ('Nearly new. Only 260,000 miles'.) Mrs Williams had an advertisement offering to exchange a wedding dress ('worn only once but has small red wine stain on the back') for a cot ('Must be sturdy'). Peter Marshall had a small advertisement for tinned goods ('Some tins slightly dented and rusted but contents almost certainly quite safe to eat. Sold at 10% off official price'). Mr Quinlan had tried to save himself an estate agency commission by putting in an advertisement for his cottage. ('Very small place. Indoor lavatory needs attention but outside lavatory functional, needs emptying once weekly or twice weekly if curry eater. Tin bath included. Stairs very narrow and steep. No view to speak of because of trees.') I wondered whether he might not have been wiser to pay the estate agent's commission after all. Mrs Tunnicliffe was advertising her late husband's collection of pipes. ('Some brand new. Mouthpieces of all used pipes wiped clean with Dettol.')

'I think I'm going to start smoking a pipe,' I said to Patsy when she appeared with two bowls of custard covered pie. I put down the parish newsletter.

She frowned.

'Mrs Tunnicliffe is selling her husband's old pipes. I thought a pipe would go nicely with the slippers, the dog and the log fire.'

Patsy smiled. 'Great idea,' she said. 'Maybe she'll have one of those curved Meerschaum pipes.'

'The sort that Sherlock Holmes used to smoke?'

'Precisely! Appropriate since Conan Doyle was a doctor. My uncle Roger used to smoke one of those. He was always setting fire to his cardigan.'

'If I get one with a big enough bowl I could have indoor bonfires. Burn old socks and unwanted magazines.'

Patsy looked at me.

'Of course, we'd have to keep the whole pipe smoking thing a secret from the patients – since I'm always telling them not to smoke.'

Patsy ignored me.

I picked up the spoon Patsy had handed me and dug into the apple pie.

I would go back to fighting the medical establishment tomorrow. Tonight I would enjoy a quiet evening with Patsy. I would enjoy the pie, the fire and my dreams.

The cats, smelling the custard, woke up. Emily was the first to move. She jumped up onto the arm of my chair and looked up at me expectantly. Ben, alerted by Emily's presence, raised his nose and also looked at me, eyes full of hope.

One of the few things I've learned in life is that when you've got a nice bowl of custard and a house full of animals, you need to keep a close eye on your custard.

The Curious Case of Mrs Groynes's Unmentionables

'We've got a pervert in the village,' said Mrs Groynes. 'One of those men who steals women's under garments.'

It had, she said, started a couple of weeks earlier.

'I noticed it when I went out into the garden to get the washing in,' she told me indignantly. 'I could see straight away that two or three bits of clothing were missing. There was a gap on the line where they'd been hung. The clothes pegs were still there but the clothes had gone. The thief had just snatched them off the line and run off with them.'

'What was missing?' I asked her.

'One of my bras and two pairs of my knickers,' she answered. 'It was my best bra. A new one. Well, nearly new. And it cost me over a pound. And he'd taken two pairs of my knickers as well.' She announced all this with some defiance; as though daring me to dispute her allegation.

'Did you see anyone take them?' I asked her, wondering why she was telling me all this.

'No, of course I didn't! If I'd seen someone take them I'd have chased him. He'd have got what for and I'd have got my things back.'

The thought of Mrs Groynes chasing someone and catching them seemed unlikely but I nodded as though this seemed the approved and likely course of action.

Sybil Groynes is a heavily built woman; put together for sturdiness and comfort rather than speed and manoeuvrability and she was probably designed by the same people who did the pyramids. She has a very small head, a huge top half and an absolutely vast bottom half. Women who are put together in these proportions are usually described as being 'pear' shaped but Mrs

Groynes did not look remotely like a pear. She looked, at best, like an artist's imaginative impression of a pear. I suspect that if she did manage to run a 100-yard sprint she would probably need to start at first light in order to complete the distance before dusk.

On the other hand, I would not like to have been a thief in possession of Mrs Groynes's unmentionables if I had been caught by her. I would imagine that she probably has a good right hook. And if she threw herself on top of you then you'd be squashed flat like a cartoon character.

In contrast, her husband Mr Sidney Groynes, is a very modestly proportioned fellow.

He has a small holding and somehow manages to scratch a living from five or six acres of fairly rough pasture land. He keeps a few pigs, a few geese, a few turkeys and a good many chickens.

The family from which Sidney Groynes comes is a remarkably large one but they have very little to do with one another.

Sidney once told me that he and the rest of the family have had so many arguments (most of which have ended in violence) that they have prepared a list of subjects they will never broach in one another's company. I once saw a copy of the list. It was seven pages long and included so many topics that I cannot imagine there was much left for them to talk about other than, perhaps, brass rubbing, slalom skiing and canoeing.

Sidney is not the brightest of God's creatures. Thumper once estimated that on the evolutionary scale he probably comes somewhere between goats and sheep. The shortage of grey matter is hereditary.

Sidney's grand-father, Evan, was born in Wales and came across the Bristol Channel on a ferry in the late 19th century; at a time when ferries commonly linked Swansea and Ilfracombe and carried thousands of tourists and workers between the two towns on a daily basis. Unfortunately, Evan was so seasick on the relatively short crossing that he vowed never to use the return half of his ticket. And nor did he. He sold it to a man from Barnstaple.

I have heard it said that Evan grew up thinking that Wales was an island and that it was not until he was in his 70s that he discovered that Wales and England are connected at the hip or, more accurately, at the northern end of the Bristol Channel and that he could, had he so wished, have made the return journey by road.

Still, long before he had made this no doubt startling and unnerving discovery, Evan had met a nice North Devon girl, got himself a job as a farm labourer, for he was by all accounts, a hard and willing worker, and started a family. They were, by all accounts, a well-matched couple for the bride, like the groom, was not an intellectual.

Sidney is Evan's grandson.

He and Sybil met at a dance in Ilfracombe. She was 16 and a bit years old and on holiday with her parents. She was, I believe, a big girl then. When her parents left to go home to Bristol, she stayed behind and moved in with Sidney. The pair married a year later when Sybil mistakenly thought she was pregnant. They never did have children and I suspect that particular ship sailed some time ago.

'Have you told the police?' I asked Sybil.

'Oh, they won't be interested,' said Mrs Groynes dismissively and, to be frank, rather contemptuously.

We used to have a policeman stationed in Bilbury but we hadn't had one of our own for a year or two. If we need a policeman we had to telephone Barnstaple. And I understood what she meant. It didn't seem likely that the Barnstaple police station would send a patrol car all the way to Bilbury to investigate the theft, or alleged theft, of three small items of feminine underwear.

'How did you think I might be able to help?' I asked.

'You know everyone in the village,' said Mrs Groynes. 'If you know any perverts just tell them that I want my undies back. If they put them back on my washing line or post them through my letterbox I won't say any more about it.'

'I'm afraid I don't know any perverts,' I told her. 'As far as I know we don't have any in Bilbury.'

'Not one?'

'Not one.'

'What about that Montgomery Hall?' demanded Mrs Groynes. 'He dresses up in women's clothes. I went past their house last summer and saw him out in the garden as large as life and twice as bold. He was sitting in a deckchair reading a book. He was wearing a frock and a straw hat. Can you imagine?' Mrs Groynes sniffed disapprovingly.

'Montgomery wouldn't steal your undies,' I told her.

The Halls live in a house called 'Dunmoanin'. He is a retired fireman and a crossdresser. He retired from the fire service suffering from stress and on his best day, he is as nervous as a kitten playing in the garden on a windy day. Montgomery Hall wouldn't have the courage to steal a bar of soap from a hotel bathroom let alone creep into someone's garden and raid her washing line.

'How do you know he wouldn't?' demanded Mrs Groynes.

'He's not your size,' I replied immediately. God could make three Montgomery Halls out of one Mrs Groynes and have enough material left over to make a five-year-old child, a small dog, a couple of cats and a handful of field mice.

Mrs Groynes thought about this. 'No, I suppose not,' she agreed reluctantly.

'I'll keep my eyes peeled,' I told her, though I didn't fancy the idea of wandering around the village demanding that every woman show me her underwear and produce the appropriate receipts.

'Hmm,' said Mrs Groynes. She folded her arms underneath her stately bosom as though she had suddenly decided that it needed more support. 'Well, if you catch them, you let me know. I'll tell my Sidney and he'll give them a good seeing to.'

I didn't think Sidney could give a 'good seeing to' to a blind tortoise but I nodded politely. 'What colour were the missing items?' I asked. I suddenly realised that I was beginning to sound like a policeman.

'The bra was white,' said Mrs Groynes. 'A size 48DD.'

What, I wondered, would a thief do with such a gargantuan item of lingerie. The thief would have to be the same size as Mrs Groynes to take full advantage of the proceeds of the crime and I doubt if there is anyone in North Devon who is the same size as Mrs Groynes.

'And the other items?' I asked.

'Both red.'

I noticed that Mrs Groynes had gone rather red herself.

She didn't give me the size of the missing knickers but it seemed reasonable to assume that they would not have found them on the rack marked 'Petite'.

'Was there anything else?' I asked. 'Anything else you need while I'm here?'

I'd driven several miles to visit Mrs Groynes at home and I hadn't expected to find myself being invited to turn into Sherlock Holmes and solve the Case of the Missing Lingerie.

'No,' said Mrs Groynes. 'Nothing else. I didn't think it was something worth bothering you about in the surgery.'

'Of course,' I said. 'Thank you.'

'Don't mention it,' said Mrs Groynes.

I got back into the Rolls and drove away.

I did not, I confess, give much thought to Mrs Groynes's missing unmentionables. I assumed that they had probably blown away in one of the gales which affect the North Devon coastline throughout the year. Or that Mrs Groynes had maybe mislaid the absent items.

Indeed, I had completely forgotten about the visit and the missing bra and undies until I happened to be passing by the Groynes's smallholding early one morning a week or so later.

I had been to visit Harry Burrows, an elderly man who lives in a cottage on the edge of Woolley Wood. Mr Burrows suffers from a dictionary of medical ailments including asthma, back trouble, high blood pressure, gallstones, early Parkinson's disease, gout, athlete's foot and chilblains. He'd called me out because he'd had a bad attack of gout.

Gout is a type of arthritis which causes severe pain. It is widely believed to affect only the big toes of elderly Colonels who have drunk too much port wine. This is nonsense, of course. In practice, I have found gout to be quite common. It affects far more men than women and it usually affects men over the age of 35 years of age. Most sufferers are overweight and a good many of them also seem to suffer with high blood pressure. Gout develops when the levels of uric acid in the blood rise too high and uric acid crystals accumulate in the joints. Any joint in the body can be affected and although it is true that the big toes are often affected, other joints which can be involved include the wrists, knees, ankles, elbows and all the joints in the fingers.

In a healthy individual, uric acid is excreted in the urine but in gout sufferers this doesn't happen properly. There are several possible reasons for this failure. In some individuals the kidneys may be damaged, and failing to get rid of uric acid properly. In others there is an inherited tendency to develop high levels of uric acid. And in a third group, which included Mr Burrows, the gout is triggered by eating too many foods which tend to produce high levels of uric acid. Foods which are particularly likely to cause gou include game, herring, whitebait, salmon, strawberries, asparagus, spinach and rhubarb. Drinks likely to cause gout (or make it worse) include port and sparkling wines such as champagne.

Mr Burrows lives on a strange diet which consisted mostly of pheasant, partridge and rhubarb. He obtains the pheasant and the partridge by trapping them in his garden (quite illegally I'm afraid) and he obtains the rhubarb by growing it next to a huge manure pile which he keeps topped up with the help of a few ponies in a neighbouring field. I had repeatedly warned him that his diet was making his gout far worse but he was stubborn and reluctant to change his diet.

'I've got a bad attack of the grout,' complained Mr Burrows, when I arrived at his cottage. He steadfastly insisted on referring to his problem as though it were a form of filler used to fill gaps between tiles or bricks. I had long ago given up trying to explain the difference.

Mr Burrows already had a supply of a non-steroidal anti-inflammatory drug and he also took allopurinol to help control the production of uric acid. It was, as usual, his left knee which was affected. I don't know why it always affects his left knee. It just does. I don't think he has ever had any trouble with his toe joints.

The knee was swollen and I injected him with a steroid. In the past this has always proved effective at reducing the swelling and the pain. I also prepared an ice pack for his knee and told him to drink plenty of water to try to flush out some of the uric acid.

I had done everything I could to help Mr Burrows and was on my way back to Bilbury Grange when I found myself driving past the Groynes' smallholding. The part of their land which they use as a garden area runs along beside the road and the hedge there is very thin and poorly kept. As I drove by, my eye was caught by something in the garden. I slowed down, came to a halt and could see that Mrs Groynes's washing was hanging on the line. She must have left it out overnight. And a huge crow was busy plucking at a large piece of red material which, when I looked more closely, was pretty obviously another pair of Mrs Groynes's knickers.

Suddenly, the crow succeeded in pulling the item of underwear from the wooden clothes peg which had been holding it on to the clothes line.

I watched in amazement as the crow then flew off, carrying Mrs Groynes's knickers.

I opened the glove compartment of the Rolls and took out a small pair of binoculars which I keep there for watching wildlife. To my astonishment, the crow took the knickers high up into a nearby sycamore tree. I could see that the bird's nest, which was largely made with the usual mixture of sticks and twigs, also contained something white and several red items. I'd heard of the red kite taking items of laundry to line a nest but I hadn't previously realised that crows had a penchant for decorating their homes with such items.

I got out of the car and knocked on the Groynes' front door.

It was Mrs Groynes herself who eventually answered my knock. She was wearing a vast and rather tatty dressing gown and had pink plastic curlers in her hair.

'I've identified the thief who took your underwear,' I told her.

'Who?' she demanded. 'I'll skin the pervert.'

'Not easy to do,' I told her.

I explained that her bra and knickers had been stolen by a crow who had used them to line a nest in a nearby tree.

She stared at me, disbelievingly.

'You can see it for yourself,' I told her. I explained where she should look. I turned to leave.

'And I'm afraid the bad news is that you've just lost another pair of your knickers,' I added. 'The crow just took a pair from your washing line.'

Mrs Groynes's immediate response was unprintable.

'Sidney!' she shouted. 'Fetch the ladder!'

I hurried back to the car, before I too was ordered to climb up the tree to retrieve the stolen undergarments.

I am proud to report that I succeeded in hiding my smile until I was out of sight.

The Mortgage Application

I know most of my patients by name. I know where they live, what they do for a living and their social circumstances. Even the individuals who haven't been to the surgery are usually well known to me because I have seen them in the village; usually at the Duck and Puddle public house or at Peter Marshall's shop.

However, I didn't recognise Mr Woodbury when he came into the surgery. And yet I could see from his medical records that he lived in the village and had done so for longer than I had. I recognised the address and I had seen Violet Woodbury, who was his wife, on a number of occasions.

Violet Woodbury is a tiny woman, if she stood on tiptoes she would probably just about measure five foot tall, and she looks rather like a neatly dressed Victorian doll. Whenever I've seen her she has always been dressed in rather old-fashioned clothes; blouses with ruffled sleeves and long skirts which reach almost to the ground. She wears her hair in those strange, old-fashioned buns – one on each side of her head so that it almost looks as if she is constantly wearing ear muffs.

Violet is a nervous, gentle woman who embroiders hand-made greeting cards which she sells to a woman who has a stall on Barnstaple Market. Peter Marshall stocks a few of her cards in his shop and I believe they sell quite well. I can't imagine how Mrs Woodbury makes any money out of the cards because the materials alone must cost her more than the prices charged for the finished articles. Each card is a small work of art and must take her several hours to complete. I've always thought it is more of a hobby than a job; something with which she keeps herself occupied when her husband is away.

I've seen her in the surgery quite a few times because she has psoriasis on her arms and legs. That is, of course, why she always wears long-sleeved blouses and long skirts.

But Farley Woodbury, her husband, was a stranger to me.

Looking at him I would have said that he was in his mid-fifties but the almost empty cardboard envelope which contained his very skimpy medical records told me that he was actually still in his mid-forties. He was, to be more precise, just 46-years-old. His face rather reminded me of Clark Gable, the film star, and he even had one of those little moustaches which Gable wore. But from the neck down he looked more like Luciano Pavarotti, the bulky Italian opera singer.

'I waited until the end of the surgery because I've got a form for you to fill in, doctor,' he said, taking a form out of his briefcase and holding it out towards me. I immediately recognised it as an insurance company document.

'My wife and I are buying a flat in London and so I've got to take out a loan from the bank,' he explained. 'The bank wants to be sure that I'm not to drop dead next week.' He shrugged and smiled. 'Or, at least, they want to feel comfortable with the odds against my dropping dead next week.'

I took the form from him and examined it. I'd seen quite a few of them.

Different companies have different forms but they're all much the same.

The first part of the form consists of a series of questions designed to elicit evidence of existing or impending ill health. The second part of the form requires the doctor to perform a number of fairly basic physical tests: pulse rate, blood pressure, weight and so on.

At the end of the whole thing the examining doctor must sign the form, either confirming that the patient is a good risk or warning the company that there is or might be a health problem which could result in a higher premium or their refusing to provide insurance cover at all.

In recompense for this work, which does not fall within a GP's commitments and responsibilities with the National Health Service, the company sends the doctor a cheque for his services. I don't see many of these forms, mainly because my practice is very small and most of the residents in Bilbury aren't about to purchase new properties or take out large loans for other purposes, but doctors with large practices in towns or cities fill in two or three of these forms a week and can make quite a bit of money out of them. My friend Will who works in general practice in the English Midlands earns enough from insurance company medicals to pay for the running of his motor car.

I do so few of them that I could probably make just about enough to keep my bicycle on the road. In practice, I give all my insurance company earnings to our local village hospital.

I am not complaining. I wouldn't swap my practice in Bilbury for a job anywhere else. And I didn't qualify as a doctor in order to fill in insurance company forms.

My questioning of Mr Woodbury didn't produce much information likely to be of interest to the insurance company. He told me that he worked as a salesman for a company making expensive yachts. His job took him all around the world and he usually spent between six and nine months of the year travelling. He had no history of serious illness, no symptoms of respiratory or cardiac problems, no joint pains and no other significant signs of illness.

'Do you have any problems with your stomach?' I asked.

'No,' he replied. 'Nothing of any great significance.'

I looked up from the form, upon which I had been putting ticks in the little boxes. I didn't say anything, just raised an eyebrow. I knew there was more.

'I get a lot of wind,' he admitted. 'I sometimes have to let my belt out a couple of notches.'

'Does the wind come up or go down when you get rid of it?'

'Both. If I'm having dinner with a client I sometimes have to excuse myself and go to the lavatory – just to let out some of the wind.' He shuffled in the chair, clearly embarrassed.

'Do you have any pain?'

'I get bad pain when the wind is at its worst. It sometimes feels as though my guts are blown up like a balloon. And the pain seems to be a result of the gut wall stretching. That's what it feels like anyway.'

'Does any particular type of food make things worse?'

'Fatty food,' said Mr Woodbury immediately.

I'd heard this before from patients. I don't think anyone knows precisely why but it seems that fatty food causes the muscles of the bowel to go into spasm. The muscular spasms then push the food through very quickly and result in the production of a mixture of mucus and diarrhoea. Patients have told me that if they eat something bland, or drink a glass of water, this sometimes helps to relieve the spasms. I suspect that the bland food merely fills up the bowels and gives the muscles something to squeeze when they go into spasm.

'Does anything help relieve the pain?'

'Eating and drinking seems to help,' said Mr Woodbury. He looked embarrassed and patted his stomach. 'Sometimes, if I've eaten a big meal and my bowels are playing up I'll make myself a sandwich – something bland and not containing much fat. A jam sandwich or something like that – together with a glass of water. If I'm staying in a hotel I'll order a salad sandwich.' He looked at me. 'It's a funny thing,' he said, 'but big hotels don't seem to stock any jam. Either that or the chefs don't know how to make a jam sandwich.'

'How often do you get the pain?'

Mr Woodbury thought for a moment. 'It varies,' he said at last. 'Sometimes I get it almost consistently for a couple of weeks. Just about every day. And then it will disappear for a few weeks.'

'Does anything else ease the pain?'

'A warm bath helps,' said Mr Woodbury. 'And I find that if I lie on my side when I'm in bed I get some relief.'

'Have you noticed whether anything makes the pain worse?'

'If I'm very stressed it can get bad,' he admitted. 'When I was young I had nerves of steel. These days the slightest aggravation seems to upset me. A friend of mine, a fellow I work with sometimes, has a theory that human beings can cope with only so much nervous strain. His idea is that the capacity for stress varies from one individual to another, but the principle remains the same for everyone. Once you've taken as much stress as you can cope with that's it – there isn't any room for any more stress.' He laughed. 'Probably sounds daft to you, doctor!'

'I've heard much dafter ideas,' I told him.

'The problem is that my job involves me meeting with some very strange people. My company sells yachts that cost £200,000 and have helicopter landing pads.' He smiled. 'Who was it who said that the rich are different to us?'

'I think it was F.Scott Fitzgerald,' I replied.

'Well, he was right,' said Mr Woodbury. 'They are different. The people I deal with are used to getting their own way. They expect you to fly half way round the world to meet them and when you get there you find that they've moved and they've flown back to where you were a day earlier. They have their own private aircraft and can fly in comfort and style but I'm flying economy on scheduled services. Plus I then have to explain to my boss why my expenses are so high and I'm not selling any boats.'

'I can see that would be very stressful,' I agreed.

He grimaced and nodded. 'Actually,' he added, 'the pain in my belly often gets worse when I'm flying – particularly if the plane is a small one. I've noticed that. I can't imagine why flying should make it worse except for the fact that when I'm in an aeroplane I'm usually rushing to be somewhere else. And for me that's a pretty stressful activity.' He looked down at his waistline. 'My size doesn't help,' he admitted. 'I don't know whether I'm imagining this but the seats on aeroplanes seem to get smaller and smaller.'

'How are your bowels?' I asked. 'When you go to the loo?'

'Fine,' he replied. 'Well, most of the time.'

I waited for him to elucidate.

'I get a bit of diarrhoea occasionally,' he explained. 'At other times I'll be constipated for a day or two.'

'Do you pass any blood with the diarrhoea? Or at any other time?'

'Oh no, nothing like that.' He paused, and looked down.

'You've looked for blood?'

'Oh yes. With all this pain I thought of the obvious.'

'Anything else?'

'It's a bit embarrassing really.'

'Go on. I'm not going to be embarrassed and you don't need to be.'

'I sometimes pass some mucus type of stuff.'

'Does that relate to the pains you get?'

'Yes, I usually get the mucus after I've had the pains.'

'Have you taken anything for the wind and the pain?'

179

'I've tried various over-the-counter medicines. I've bought several medicines recommended for flatulence. I've been to a few pharmacists and asked them for stuff. I've tried stuff in the States, in Japan, in Germany and here.'

'Has any of it helped?'

'A little bit. But not a lot.'

'But you do find that the wind and the bowel problems are caused or made worse by what you eat?'

'Oh yes, definitely. If I eat something that is very fatty then I'm usually bad for a few days afterwards. I try to avoid fatty foods as much as I can but in my job it isn't always easy. I have to eat out with clients and because the people who buy the sort of yachts I sell are pretty rich I have to take them somewhere expensive. And posh restaurants and hotels seem to serve a lot of very fatty food.'

I nodded, made a few notes on a notepad which I keep on my desk but I didn't write anything on the form for the time being.

'Pop behind the screen and undress down to your underwear,' I told him. I looked at the form. 'I need to examine you and this particular insurance company seems to want a pretty thorough examination.'

'The bank is lending us quite a chunk of money,' explained Mr Woodbury. 'We're buying a flat in Kensington. It'll mean that my wife can stay in London with me when I have to see clients in the city. She prefers staying here in Bilbury but at the moment I sometimes go for a month or six weeks without seeing her. Having a flat in town will mean that we can spend a few days together when I'm seeing potential customers.' He pulled a face. 'Property in London is ridiculously expensive but we're hoping it will be an investment.'

'I'm sure it will be!' I said.

'We're having to pay £20,000 for quite a small flat!' said Mr Woodbury. 'One bedroom, living room, dining room and bathroom and kitchen.'

I looked at him, astonished. '£20,000 for a flat!'

'I know,' he said. 'Ridiculous, isn't it? You can buy quite a large house in Bilbury for less than that.'

I couldn't help wondering if property prices in London could go much higher than they had already reached. In my innocence and ignorance, it seemed impossible that Mr Woodbury would be able to make money on his investment. But that, of course, was not my problem.

He stood up and went behind the screen.

While he undressed I looked at the rest of the form, and thought about what I'd learned.

I was convinced, from the story he'd told me, that Mr Woodbury was suffering from a disorder known as irritable bowel syndrome.

Back in the 19th century, irritable bowel syndrome, or IBS, used to be known as 'spastic colon'. Back then no one really knew what caused it or why the bowel muscles went into such painful spasms. A hundred years later, in the 1970s, and still no one knew what caused it or why the bowel muscles went into such powerful and painful spasms.

It is a debilitating and underestimated disorder and the name, which makes the disorder sound almost insignificant, really doesn't do it justice. Because it doesn't kill those who suffer from it, doctors don't tend to take it very seriously and researchers have generally avoided doing any work to find out more about it.

Doctors also tend to be suspicious about diseases which produce only symptoms – they tend to think of really serious, deadly diseases as producing lots of measurable signs.

But my experience as a GP had taught me that IBS can wreck people's lives. And there is certainly no doubt that the pain caused by the muscle cramping associated with IBS can be among the most incapacitating of all pains.

But IBS is not considered to be a life threatening disorder and the insurance company form contained no box for me to report this condition.

'Do you want me to lie down on the couch?' Mr Woodbury asked, now wearing just his vest, underpants and socks. He was clearly grossly overweight and I suspected that either his suit had been handmade to try to disguise his weight or else he had been wearing some sort of corset to hold in his tummy. If he'd been female I'd have suspected that he was about to deliver a brace of bouncing new twins.

Apart from his being considerably overweight, my physical examination didn't produce anything much of interest. His blood pressure was surprisingly normal. His lungs were clear. His heart was ticking away very nicely. His joints all worked perfectly well. There were no signs of any neurological problems. His eyesight was normal. His hearing was excellent. He had no enlarged glands. His teeth and mouth were fine.

When I examined his abdomen I could feel nothing abnormal, though to be honest he was so overweight that the examination was a little difficult to do thoroughly. I put a finger into his back passage and found no signs of an enlarged prostate or any other abnormality. He had no enlarged lymph nodes. His temperature was entirely normal. His skin was free of serious blemishes and except for a rather bad fungal infection between the toes and on the nails of both feet, I could find nothing wrong there. As far as I know, no one has ever died of athlete's foot so I didn't consider that discovery to be of any great significance.

I gave him my usual little talk about the need to lose weight. I told him that I understood why he ate too much but I warned him that if he didn't lose weight then the excess he was carrying would have a long-term damaging effect on his heart, his joints and just about every other part of his body. I gave him a calorie booklet I'd had printed. It contains details of how many calories different foods contain. And I gave him another leaflet which contains my dieting tips.

Mr Woodbury looked suitably contrite and promised to make a real effort to lose some weight.

Finally, I told him that I needed a urine sample. I told him to get dressed, gave him a sample bottle and told him where he would find our downstairs cloakroom.

While I waited for him to produce a sample, I continued to fill in the form the insurance company had provided. I have never been very good at filling in forms. I don't know why it is but I often find myself rushing and missing a box here or there. And then, two weeks later, the form comes back to me with a note explaining what I've forgotten and asking me to finish the job I've started.

And so I always take special care when filling in an insurance medical form for a patient. I know that an error can lead to a delay in them obtaining the money they need and, consequently, a delay in completing their property purchase. I am very well aware that the whole property buying chain is complicated enough without me making it any worse.

Moments later Mr Woodbury returned, handed me the usual, warm plastic bottle and sat down. I took the bottle over to the sink in the corner of my consulting room where I perform tests of this type. I dipped one of the little indicator sticks into the urine. These little paper sticks have revolutionised medical practice. They were the one aspect of medical practice which my predecessor Dr Brownlow found most useful. He claimed that as far as he was concerned nothing, absolutely nothing, had revolutionised his life quite as much as the little paper testing sticks. In his earlier career, the testing of urine had involved much glassware and a good deal of expertise.

In the old days, a doctor would need real laboratory equipment to test to see if there was any blood or sugar in a urine sample. And testing to see if a woman was pregnant would require a good deal of patience.

These days a doctor can tell if there is sugar or blood in a urine sample within a couple of minutes.

I really didn't expect to see any abnormality when I tested Mr Woodbury's urine. There was absolutely no reason to suspect that there might be any positive result at all.

And so I was startled when the little slip of paper I was using showed that there was a trace of blood in Mr Woodbury's urine sample. To be honest 'startled' is not a strong enough word. I was actually quite shocked and horrified. It was not something I expected and I was pretty sure it was not something that Mr Woodbury could have suspected.

I was so shocked that I repeated the test with another testing stick. This too produced a positive result.

The amount of blood in his urine wasn't great. But the test was nevertheless definitive. Mr Woodbury had blood in his urine. And blood in the urine is not something that can, or should, be ignored.

I poured the rest of the urine down the sink, threw the empty bottle and the two testing strips into the pedal operated waste bin underneath the sink, and went back to my chair. The diagnosis of IBS which I had already made now seemed very insignificant.

'Everything OK, doctor?' asked Mr Woodbury. Like me he clearly did not expect the test to produce any evidence of importance.

'I'm afraid your urine isn't quite as clear as I would like,' I told him. 'I need to arrange a couple of tests at the hospital in Barnstaple.'

Mr Woodbury looked at me and paled noticeably. 'What sort of tests?' he asked. 'What's the problem?'

It is bad enough when a patient visits a doctor with signs or symptoms and then is told that the symptoms of which he has complained, or the signs which he has noticed, are as significant as he may have feared.

(Symptoms, of course, are the physical or mental features of a disorder which are apparent to the patient whereas signs are the physical or mental features which usually have to be elicited by the doctor. So, for example, a headache or blurred vision is a symptom whereas a heart murmur or an exaggerated neurological reflex is a sign.)

But it is, I suspect, worse when a patient who feels perfectly healthy visits a doctor for an entirely routine examination and is told that there is a problem with his or her health. To hear that there is a problem, under these circumstances, must be quite a shock. There has been no time for the patient to prepare himself, or herself, for bad news.

'There was a tiny amount of blood in your urine,' I told him.

I prefer to be honest with patients when I can.

I think it can sometimes be worse if a patient is left in the dark and allowed to imagine all sorts of strange scenarios. Unless there are obvious signs to the contrary, I like to assume that my patients are not stupid. And I am certainly aware that if a doctor tries to hide the truth then there is a real risk that the patient will go away convinced of the worst. It is not unknown for patients who have very curable problems to commit suicide because they were allowed to harbour unnecessary fears.

'There wasn't enough for me to see any sign of blood in the urine with the naked eye,' I told him. 'But the testing strip found a small amount of blood.' I paused. 'A very small amount,' I added.

'What do you think the problem could be?' asked Mr Woodbury.

'I don't know,' I told him honestly. 'There are lots of possible causes of blood in the urine. You haven't had an injury recently, have you? Been hit or kicked in the kidneys?'

'No, definitely not,' said Mr Woodbury.

'You don't do any strenuous exercise?'

Mr Woodbury laughed rather wryly. 'Do I look like a man who does any strenuous exercise.'

I smiled my understanding. 'Do you have any stinging when you pass urine?'

'No, nothing like that.'

Blood in the urine can be caused by a urinary tract infection but this seemed unlikely. The testing strip I had used had shown no sign of any infection and the urine sample had looked perfectly clear.

'Have you had any discharge from your penis? Any signs of an infection there?'

Mr Woodbury shook his head.

'Let me take a look,' I said, standing up.

Mr Woodbury stood up too, and unbuttoned his trousers so that I could examine his penis and scrotum. There were absolutely no abnormalities. No lumps, no rash, no sores and no visible bleeding.

'Could it be cancer?' asked Mr Woodbury bluntly, after he'd sat down and while I was washing my hands.

'It's a possibility we have to exclude,' I told him.

'What sort of cancer could it be?'

'Cancer of the bladder is one possibility and cancer of the kidney is another,' I told him. 'But there is probably a much simpler explanation. And even if there is a cancer, it is clearly very early on because the amount of blood in your urine is very, very small.'

'How soon can you arrange the tests?' asked Mr Woodbury.

'I'll fix it up now,' I told him.

Patients who live in big cities invariably have access to much bigger and better equipped hospitals than the ones available in rural areas. But there are more likely to be waiting lists for essential tests in big hospitals.

One of the advantages of being in a fairly lowly populated area such as North Devon is that it is often perfectly possible to arrange an appointment for tests to be done the same day or the next day.

I picked up the telephone and telephoned the local X-ray department.

'Can you get to the hospital in Barnstaple this afternoon?' I asked Mr Woodbury, holding my hand over the telephone.

'Today?' Mr Woodbury seemed shocked by the speed of the appointment.

'Yes.'

I took my hand off the mouthpiece, fixed a time and then replaced the telephone.

'Be at the X-ray department at three o' clock this afternoon,' I told him. 'They'll do some tests for me. And then come back to see me at this evening's surgery. I'll speak to the radiologist when he's seen you and I should have some news for you by then.'

'I don't need an appointment to see you this evening?'

'No, of course not – you just have to turn up at the surgery. I don't have an appointments system for any of my surgeries.'

Mr Woodbury thanked me and, still looking rather pale, left.

I looked at my watch. Mr Woodbury's insurance medical examination had taken quite a while and it was now nearly 1 p.m. I checked the list of home visits which Miss Johnson had put on my desk before Mr Woodbury's consultation.

There were just two visits to do and neither of them was urgent. I decided to have my lunch and then do the visits after I had eaten.

One of the many things I have learned as a GP working in a solitary practice is that it is always wise to eat when you can.

On too many occasions I have put off having my lunch, spent the whole afternoon doing fairly routine home visits, returned to Bilbury Grange to do the evening surgery, had to go out on an urgent visit when I should have been eating my dinner and found myself eating my first food for more than twelve hours at 10 o'clock at night.

So I joined Patsy and we had a light lunch of soup, and a couple of sandwiches made with fresh home-made bread and some excellent local cheddar cheese. The cheese is made by a farmer who is a patient of mine and who brings us a block of the stuff every weekend as a 'thank you' for services rendered.

In the afternoon, I completed the two visits and then caught up on some paperwork. Even back in the 1970s, general practitioners spent a good deal of their lives dealing with paperwork.

Mr Woodbury returned to Bilbury Grange that evening.

He came to the surgery with his wife, Violet, and explained that after the morning consultation he had gone straight home and told his wife that he needed to go to the hospital. She had gone with him and waited while he was in the X-ray department.

Unlike the morning, when he had generously waited until the end of the surgery because he suspected that his appointment was going to take longer than everyone else's, he was the first to appear in the surgery. He wanted to know the news. And who wouldn't?

I had got off the telephone to the radiologist just half an hour earlier and I had spent that thirty minutes thinking about Mr Woodbury's condition.

Hospitals are bound up with a lot of red tape and there are frequently long administrative delays in getting the results of X-rays and laboratory results to the GP. The result can be that patients sometimes have to wait weeks to find out whether or not they have a serious disease. This delay inevitably means that starting essential treatment will necessarily be delayed. And that can be fatal. I have always preferred to telephone the hospital and speak to the doctor who did the tests and who can give me the information first hand, without waiting for it to come through the post.

For both the doctor and the patient this is one of the advantages of living in a fairly remote rural village. A city GP, with two or three thousand patients to look after, probably wouldn't have time to ring the hospital. And even if he found the time he would probably have great difficulty finding the doctor who had conducted the tests.

Our local Barnstaple hospital has a small number of staff. I know most of them personally and so I can ring up, speak directly to them and get the information I need.

Just ten minutes earlier I had suddenly realised that I had had, all the time, two valuable pieces of information which I'd missed.

The Woodburys came into the surgery holding hands. They were both white with anxiety.

'You can stop worrying,' I told them both, before they had even sat down. I hate doctors who behave as though they are conducting a quiz show, and who make patients wait for ages before they give them the news they have been waiting for. I once worked for a hospital consultant who would make patients wait four or five minutes before giving them the important information which they had been so desperate to receive.

'The radiologist is certain that there is no cancer in your bladder or either of your kidneys,' I told Mr Woodbury.' As you know, the hospital did X-rays of your bladder and both kidneys and they looked at everything with their ultrasound equipment. They also did some blood tests. And the radiologist, who is an excellent doctor, is quite certain that you don't have cancer of the bladder or cancer of the kidneys.'

Mrs Woodbury burst into tears. Mr Woodbury put his arm around her and gave her a hug.

I busied myself with some paperwork on my desk, giving them both time to take in the good news and settle a little.

'Do they have any idea what caused the bleeding?' asked Mr Woodbury. He coughed to clear his throat. His voice was wavering.

'No, they don't,' I told him. 'We've ruled out all the usual, obvious causes. There is no growth and no infection. But just before you got here I was thinking about everything you told me and I think I know what caused the blood in your urine.'

They both looked at me, expectantly.

'When we talked this morning you told me that your abdominal pain and swelling got worse when you were travelling in aeroplanes,' I said.

Mr Woodbury nodded. 'That's right.'

'I'm pretty sure that the swelling and the pain are symptoms of irritable bowel syndrome,' I told him. 'And the pain in your abdomen gets worse when you're flying because the gases in the intestinal tract expand at higher altitudes.'

They both nodded.

'That makes sense,' said Mr Woodbury.

The radiologist had inadvertently helped with the diagnosis because he had told me that when he looked at the X-rays of Mr Woodbury's kidneys, he could hardly see anything because of the amount of gas in the intestine. No X-ray report would have contained such valuable information.

'Irritable bowel syndrome often seems to get worse when sufferers eat fatty food,' I explained. 'I have no idea why. But it is, nevertheless, a fact. For most people this is actually quite good for their health because folk who eat less fatty food are less likely to develop circulatory problems – heart disease and strokes – and are also less likely to develop cancer.'

'But how does that relate to the blood in my urine?'

'When the wind inside your intestine expands it presses on the other organs inside your abdomen,' I explained. 'And my theory is that it is the pressure on one or both of your kidneys which has caused the bleeding.'

'But could wind do that?' asked Mrs Woodbury.

'I don't see why not,' I replied. 'If the kidney is bruised or knocked hard then it is quite common to find blood in the urine. So if the kidney is under pressure from a wind-filled length of intestine, it makes sense to me that there might be some bleeding. Don't forget that there were only microscopic amounts of blood in your husband's urine.'

'That sounds as if it would be good news,' said Mr Woodbury.

'Certainly,' I said. 'It then leaves us with the problem of dealing with your irritable bowel syndrome – rather than the problem of dealing with a kidney problem. And that's much simpler because IBS is far less threatening than a kidney cancer.'

'Is there a test that you can do to check this out?' asked Mr Woodbury. 'To see if your diagnosis is the right one?'

'There isn't a specific test,' I told him. 'And I have to tell you that this is my own theory. I've never seen it discussed by other doctors as an explanation for blood in the urine.'

'But you've thought of a test?'

I nodded. 'There's a very simple test we can do,' I said to Mr Woodbury. 'You come back and see me when you haven't got much wind in your intestines – on a day when your irritable bowel syndrome isn't causing you any trouble.'

'And you'll test my husband's urine?' said Mrs Woodbury.

'Absolutely right.'

'And if there's no blood in my urine then the chances are that your diagnosis is the right one?'

'Yes.'

'How can I get my irritable bowel syndrome under control?' asked Mr Woodbury.

'Try to avoid stress for a few days, take things easy and make sure you avoid foods which you know tend to give you wind. Do you have to go flying off anywhere over the next few days?'

'No,' said Mrs Woodbury. She was very definite. 'Farley is taking some time off. While he was being X-rayed, I used a pay phone at the hospital and telephoned his boss. I told them that Farley wouldn't be at work for a while. They were very good about it and told him to take as much time off as he needed. He's got a month's holiday that he hasn't used and he hasn't been off sick for years.'

'Splendid,' I said. 'Then you come back and see me again in a few days when you're happy that there isn't so much wind in your abdomen.'

'And you'll do another urine test,' added Mrs Woodbury.

'Exactly,' I agreed.

They both stood up and Mrs Woodbury thanked me for getting the results so quickly. 'My friend lives in Birmingham,' she said, 'and she had to wait three weeks for the results of her X-ray. She was on tenterhooks the whole time. So we both appreciate what you've done.'

I pointed out that it is much easier to get hospital results quickly when you live and work in a small community. And I told them that I looked forward to seeing Mr Woodbury as soon as he felt that he was ready for another urine test.

It was five days before Mr Woodbury returned to Bilbury Grange.

He and his wife came into the evening surgery. They were holding hands again.

'As you suggested, I've come to have another urine test,' said Mr Woodbury, after they had sat down.

'No wind?' I asked.

'None,' said Mr Woodbury. 'But I had a bad 48 hours after that day when I saw you and went to the hospital. The pain was as bad as it has ever been.'

'I wanted to call you,' said Mrs Woodbury, looking at her husband. 'His tummy was terribly swollen. But Farley said he just wanted to rest and wait for the wind to subside.'

'It may not look as if it has, but my tummy has gone down a lot,' said Mr Woodbury, patting his abdomen.

I stood up and fetched a urine bottle from the cupboard where I keep such things. I handed the bottle to Mr Woodbury who stood up to take the bottle from me. His wife didn't want to let go of his hand. 'You know what to do,' I told him.

'Do you think everything will be all right?' asked Mrs Woodbury when her husband had left the consulting room to put a sample of urine into the bottle. Her voice was quavering. She was clearly very nervous.

'He hasn't got cancer,' I told her. 'All this is going to do is show us if my guess is correct. If there isn't any blood in your husband's urine then I was almost certainly correct in thinking that the bleeding was caused by the swollen bowel pressing on one of his kidneys. But if there is still some blood there then my guess could still be right – and we'll just have to repeat the test in a few more days' time. Either way, I really don't think there is any reason for you to be worried.'

Mrs Woodbury licked her lips and nodded. She didn't say anything.

'So remember: even if there is blood in his urine, there really isn't anything for you to worry about,' I told her. 'We all tend to put too much emphasis on tests. The important thing is the way your husband feels and how he looks. And there are absolutely no important signs of anything for us to be worried about.'

Mrs Woodbury nodded again. I have to say that she did not look convinced by my attempt to reassure her.

A moment later Mr Woodbury returned carrying the little plastic bottle which contained his sample. I told him to sit down while I did the necessary with one of my little testing strips.

I did it twice. Just to make sure.

'It's clear,' I told them both. 'Perfectly clear. There's no trace of any blood in the urine sample.'

Mrs Woodbury started to cry. Mr Woodbury put his arm around her and looked very relieved.

'So you were right about the wind in my bowel pressing on my kidneys?'

'I think so,' I said. I opened the top drawer of my desk and took out the insurance form I had almost completed. 'I hope you don't mind,' I said, 'but I kept this back for a day or two so that I could put in a note about your urine being clear. I don't think there's any need for us to mention the other test or the X-rays. The insurance company doesn't ask about things like that. They're only interested in things that are wrong; problems that might cost them money.'

Mr Woodbury and his wife looked at each other. 'We aren't going ahead with the purchase,' said Mr Woodbury. 'So I'm afraid we won't need the mortgage, or the loan or the insurance company form.'

I looked at them and raised a questioning eyebrow. I have to admit that I was surprised.

'Farley has given in his notice,' explained Mrs Woodbury. 'He's found a job at a small boatyard just outside Bideford. They make small sailing boats for weekend sailors and they've been looking for a marketing manager. It'll involve a little bit of travel, but only in the West Country and there won't be any foreign travel or trips to London.' She looked very pleased with the way things had turned out.

'I feel very good about it,' said Mr Woodbury.

'So we won't need that ridiculously expensive flat in London,' said Mrs Woodbury. 'We've rung the bank and cancelled the arrangement. They were very understanding about it.'

'It'll mean quite a cut in my salary,' said Mr Woodbury. 'And there are no big bonuses. But there's a possibility of a seat on the board in two years' time and if things go satisfactorily for us all then they'll let me put a little of our money into the business. The owner is in his 70s and his children aren't in the slightest bit interested in running a boatyard.'

There are quite a few boatyards in North Devon and I have patients working in several of them. I knew the boatyard he was talking about and I thought he was probably right: the owner's children didn't live in Devon and I couldn't imagine them ever wanting to make boats for a living.

'We think it's the right thing for us,' said Mrs Woodbury. 'Farley can come home every evening and I can make sure he sticks to his diet and cuts out any foods that upset his tummy.'

'None of those rich, fatty sauces,' said Mr Woodbury.

'Absolutely not!' said Mrs Woodbury.

'So, I'm sorry to have wasted your time with the form,' said Mr Woodbury.

'But it all turned out for the best,' said Mrs Woodbury.

I congratulated them both on their decision, told them I thought that they'd done a brave and wise thing and wished them well for the future.

They stood up, still holding hands.

'One final thing,' I said to Mr Woodbury. 'Now that you're living in the village full time, I want to see you once a month so that I can weigh you.'

'We've got some scales in our bathroom,' said Mrs Woodbury.

'I'm sure you have,' I said. 'But the scales won't tell your husband off if he isn't losing weight. Knowing that he has to come here once a month might just add a little extra bite to his incentive to lose weight.'

Mr Woodbury smiled and nodded.

When they'd gone, I picked up the now unwanted insurance form. It was completed and ready to go off to the company which had commissioned it. They'd even provided me with a stamped addressed envelope so that I could send it back to them. I dropped the form and the envelope into my waste basket.

The waste basket looked a suitable resting place for it.

And then I looked at the form for a moment and thought about it.

The insurance company had commissioned the report. It only seemed fair that they should pay me for the work I had done. The cheque would, after all, go into our cottage hospital's bank account. It wasn't my fault that the insurance report was no longer required.

It was the work of a moment to sign the form, slip it into its envelope and put it into the 'Out' tray on my desk.

Miss Johnson would give it to the postman to take away.

I pressed the buzzer for the next patient to come in.

One of the joys of general practice is that you never know who is going to walk through the door – and what their problem is going to be.

One thing is certain: life as a country GP is never dull.

Finally…

I hope you have enjoyed this book. If you did so then I would be enormously encouraged if you would spare a moment to write a short review.

Thank you

Vernon Coleman

Appendix One

The Freedom of Bilbury

It was decided at the last meeting of the Bilbury Parish Council that readers who have read all ten Bilbury books are entitled to hold the Freedom of Bilbury, North Devon, England and to list this honour on their curriculum vitae, visiting cards and proclamations.

Those who hold the Freedom of Bilbury are also entitled to:

Ride a horse through the lanes of Bilbury on the first Tuesday in Lent.

Graze up to 12 sheep or goats on Bilbury Common for up to 60 days a year.

Be an honorary Life Vice President of Bilbury Cricket Club. Vice Presidents are guaranteed a deckchair at all home matches and unlimited supplies of tea, sandwiches and cake (three varieties usually available but not guaranteed). They are also entitled to describe themselves (on CVs, biographies, etc.) as being a Life Vice President of Bilbury Cricket Club.

Hold honorary life membership of Peter Marshall's Vegetable of the Month Club. Members are entitled to purchase the Vegetable of the Month with a 2% discount on shop prices. Members will receive a free brown paper bag with their first order. For full rules and conditions please see the notice pinned up at the back of Peter Marshall's shop (just behind the shelf containing the tinned apricots and the tinned dog food).

Vote in all elections held in Bilbury.

Enjoy a guaranteed reserved seat in Bilbury Church on the occasions of both the Harvest Festival and the Christmas Carol Service. (Not behind a pillar.) No large, wedding style hats, please.

Enjoy a 10% discount on the price of all sandwiches and beverages (alcoholic and non-alcoholic) served at the Duck and Puddle public house in Bilbury.

Attend the Annual Guy Fawkes Celebration Fireworks Night Party on November 5th every year and receive a complimentary baked potato with full access to the condiments tray.

Receive two tickets for all productions staged by the Bilbury Amateur Dramatics Society and two back stage passes to the After Show 'Meet the Cast' Drinks Party. (Drinks to be paid for separately).

Purchase a family plot (suitable for 4 lying or 8 standing) in Bilbury graveyard. For details of prices and full terms and conditions please contact Peter Marshall (official agent for the vicar). A 6% discount on all funerals and headstones arranged through Peter Marshall is also available.

Appendix Two

Bilbury Parish Newsletter: Classified Advertisement Section

At the end of the memory entitled 'Paula Temple' I mentioned the Bilbury Newsletter. Here is a sample selection of advertisements taken from the Classified Advertising Section of the Newsletter.

* Chiropodist: for all your foot problems. Specialities include warts, veruccas, dry skin, athletes foot. All dealt with while you wait. No appointments necessary unless I am busy. Fees very reasonable. Discount for pensioners. Contact Gladys Periwinkle at Rose Cottage. If you call and I am out just let yourself in, make a cup of tea while you wait.

* Antique Victorian Ottoman. Unique. Rumoured to have been sat on by Conan Doyle and Prince Albert (though not at the same time). Last three available. Contact Patchy Fogg on Bilbury 127.

* Bilbury Garage: We have a repaired second-hand exhaust pipe from Ford Poplar for sale. Probably has a few miles left in it. Can adapt and weld to just about any make of car. £8.10 including fitting. Telephone Bilbury 114.

* Odd Jobs: Man with experience prepared to tackle difficult jobs involving grass and similar. Do you have grass which needs cutting or hedge which needs trimming? Contact Harry Burrows in bar at Duck and Puddle any morning, afternoon or evening. Will also cut hair, clean drains and shampoo dogs which do not bite.

* Peter Marshall: Sandwiches special offer for busy people. Let me make your sandwiches for you. You pay only for the slice of bread on the bottom. The slice of bread on the top is FREE. Choose any filling you like from fish paste, raspberry jam or cheese. Please note: despite malicious rumours being spread by certain parties who know who they are I do wash both hands before preparing

sandwiches. Note: Bilbury doctor has confirmed that last month's unfortunate outbreak of food poisoning could have been a result of mistaken use of fishpaste from old stock.

* Church Sewing Group: meets every Monday except when choir is practising.

* Women's Institute: Next meeting will be on 3rd Wednesday of month as usual. Mrs Bertha Aldridge will again give talk on her 1962 visit to 'The Belgian Industrial Heartlands' and Mr Charles Aldridge will once more show his prize winning slides. Admission free.

* Choir: rehearsals every Monday except when Church sewing group is meeting.

* Bell ringing: The Bilbury hand bell ringing group will meet at the Duck and Puddle on the last Thursday of the month. Unfortunately, but understandably in view of the unfortunate incident last month, Frank and Gilly Parsons have, on the advice of their insurers, ruled that we can no longer ring our bells inside the pub. If the weather is clement we will therefore ring bells in field across road from pub. The one with the black and white cows in it. Permission has been requested, reply is pending. Ringers (especially Elspeth Jackson) are requested to keep firm hold on their bells at all times. (We are pleased to say that Albert Treadwell is reported to be making a good recovery from his unfortunate injury.) Please tread carefully when in field. If weather is inclement we will meet in Duck and Puddle and do silent bell ringing with noises made orally (by mouth). Those whose surnames begin with A to M do 'dongs'. Those with surnames beginning N to Z do 'dings'. For more information contact Olive Robinson (Hon Sec) Telephone: Bilbury 109

* 11 jars of fishpaste for sale. Unused. Apply Peter Marshall shop.

* Television for sale. Does not work at moment. But vet in Combe Martin (whose cousin has similar model) says it probably only needs new valves. All buttons still present and nice cabinet in fair condition. Stain on top of cabinet can easily be covered with medium sized doily. Looks impressive. Sensible offers considered. Telephone: Samuel Houghton on Bilbury 82 and ask for message to be taken to Josh Wilkins. (No messages delivered after 8 p.m.)

* Gravedigger's Rest public house, Barnstaple: Entertainment Thursday evenings and Saturday lunchtimes. Birthday groups catered for but no celebrations for over 60s without medical certificate please. Please note that patrons who catch items of clothing discarded by artistes are requested to return them to the management.

* Duck and Puddle public house. Food available at mealtimes or between if necessary. Fire lit when weather cold.

* Memorial service for Fred Pilbury (who celebrated 65th birthday at the Gravedigger's Rest, Barnstaple last Tuesday and died suddenly and unexpectedly) will be held next Wednesday at the Gravedigger's Rest, Barnstaple. 'He went with a smile on his face'.

* Windows cleaned : Price 10 pence per window. Ground floor windows only please as a result of recent fall. Phone Bilbury 45 and ask for Edward.

* Sweep: Telephone Bilbury 73 to book a good luck sweep to attend your next wedding. Will pose for photographs and kiss bride (and bridesmaids) if required. Ring same number for appointment to sweep your chimney.

* Cottage for sale: Parlour, kitchen, two bedrooms. Tin bath. Water from well in garden. Well has never dried up except in 1934, 1957, 1965, 1966 and 1967. Outdoor water closet. No electricity. Low ceilings so property probably suit smaller person. Barn suitable for small horse and very small cart. Strawberry patch produces fruit annually if netted. Telephone Bilbury 87 for details and appointment to view.

* Long wooden ladder for sale. Suitable for cleaning first floor windows, gutters, etc. Most rungs still present. Phone Bilbury 45 and ask for Doreen. Buyer to collect.

* Stop Press: Choir practice is moved to Tuesdays until further notice unless alternative arrangements made.

* Stop Press: Church sewing group is moved to Tuesdays to avoid clash with choir. However, we would like to point out that we had been meeting on Mondays for longer than the choir.

Appendix Three

Benzodiazepines: a little background

I first started drawing attention to the horrors of benzodiazepines (drugs such as Valium, Ativan and Mogadon) back in the early 1970s. I drew attention to the problem in my book *The Medicine Men* in 1975 and was vilified by the medical profession for doing so.

In the two decades which followed, I wrote hundreds of articles about these drugs. I also spoke widely to warn doctors and patients of their addictive nature. I made scores of television programmes and in the early 1980s I recorded a series of special radio programmes dealing with benzodiazepine addiction. At the same time I also wrote and distributed a newsletter on benzodiazepine addiction. Mail from readers was arriving at my home in grey sacks.

Thousands of patients wrote in to me to say that their lives had been ruined by benzodiazepines.

At that time (and I remember this very well) the British Medical Association seemed able to find an endless parade of doctors prepared to go on radio or television and tell the world that I was a dangerous, scaremongering lunatic. The BMA and the medical establishment stood shoulder to shoulder with the pharmaceutical industry in defence of these awful medicines. This is perhaps not surprising – after all, the BMA's in-house journal (the *British Medical Journal*) was earning zillions in advertising revenue from the drug companies.

I have dealt with benzodiazepines at some length in a number of my medical books (notably *The Medicine Men* (1975), *Life Without Tranquillisers* (1985), *Addicts and Addictions* (1986) and *The Drugs Myth* (1992).

Sadly, many doctors still refuse to accept that these drugs are a real problem. And so here, below, is a short analysis of the history of benzodiazepines and a list of some of the evidence which illustrates the size of the problem. The material on the list below is taken from my own books.

The Valium story began in the 1930s when Dr Leo H Sternbach was working as a research assistant at the University of Krakow in Poland. He was investigating benzophenones and heptoxdiazines.

Dr Sternbach continued work on these substances in 1954 in the New Jersey laboratories of Hoffman La Roche. The result of his last experiment was called Ro5-0690 and was shelved as of little interest.

In 1957, Ro5-0690 was submitted for testing by Roche's Director of Pharmacological Research and a report was published showing that the drug was a hypnotic, a sedative and a muscle relaxant. It was a new chemical substance.

In late 1958, Roche did more tests on the drug and found that it was effective at treating anxiety and tension. The drug was called chlordiazepoxide.

On February 24th 1960, the American Food and Drug Administration approved the drug which was launched a few weeks later as Librium.

Before the end of 1960 other drug companies, Include Wyeth Laboratories had introduced benzodiazepines of their own.

In 1961, a clinical report appeared in the journal *Psyschopharmacologia* which warned that patients were becoming addicted to chlordiazepoxide.

By the early 1960s, GPs were prescribing these drugs for an enormous range of physical and mental problems. It is difficult to think of a medical condition for which benzodiazepines were not prescribed.

In 1968, a paper in the *Journal of the American Medical Association* showed that benzodiazepines caused depression and suicidal thoughts.

In 1970 in a book called *Discoveries in Biological Psychiatry*, edited by Ayd and Blackell, Frank Ayd wrote: 'Although vast quantities of minor tranquillisers have been prescribed it must be stated that not all have been dispensed judiciously by some practitioners. Such misuse is indicative of physicians who unwisely accede to the demands of patients or who supplant sound clinical judgement or expediency'.

In 1972, the *American Journal of Psychiatry* published a paper describing how patients on diazepam had exhibited symptoms which included apprehension, insomnia and depression. The patients had previously been emotionally stable. When the patients were taken off the drugs, their symptoms disappeared.

In 1973, I organised a symposium at the Royal Society of Medicine. It was stated that when patients were taken off their benzodiazepines they often felt much better than they had felt for years. The symposium was organised on behalf of the *British Clinical Journal* which I was editing. I immediately began writing articles about benzodiazepines for the national press.

In 1975, the *British Medical Journal* published an editorial referring to an article published in the *Lancet* in 1960 which had reported that a patient taking chordiazepoxide had assaulted his wife – the first sign of aggression in 20 years of marriage.

In 1979, the WHO estimated that there were 700 different benzodiazepines on the market. These drugs were the most widely prescribed in the world. It was generally agreed that there was no real difference in any of the drugs – they were all equally effective and equally troublesome.

In 1979, the *Journal of the Royal Society of Medicine* published a report showing that poisoning with tranquillisers and sleeping tablets accounted for 61,000 hospital admissions each year.

If you went to see a GP in 1970, you had a better than one in twenty chance that you would come away with a prescription for a benzodiazepine. By 1977, one in five people who was given a prescription was given a prescription for one of these drugs. Among women in the 45 to 59 age group, one in three was given a tranquilliser of some sort.

In my first book *The Medicine Men* (1975) I predicted that doctors would end up trying to wean patients off benzodiazepines.

In 1975, three doctors from the Drug Dependence Treatment Center at the Philadelphia VA Hospital published a paper entitled *Misuse and Abuse of Diazepam: An Increasingly Common Medical Problem*. The paper referred back to papers published as far back as 1970 which had documented instances of physical addiction to benzodiazepines. The paper concluded: 'All physicians should know that diazepam abuse and misuse is occurring and careful attention should be given to prescribing, transporting and storing this drug.'

In 1979, a psychiatrist testifying to a US Senate health sub-committee claimed that patients could become hooked on diazepam in six weeks. Another witness said it was harder to kick benzodiazepines than to get off heroin. A third witness said that tranquillisers were America's second biggest addiction problem – after alcoholism.

In 1979, the *British Medical Journal* reported a study involving over 40,000 patients. The paper showed 'a highly significant association between the use of minor tranquillisers and the risk of a serious road accident'.

In 1981, at a meeting of the American Association for the Advancement of Science, it was suggested that diazepam might be linked to cancer. It was argued that women whose breast cancers had developed more quickly had been taking diazepam.

In 1982, a British Professor of Psychopharmacology reported that brain scans showed that patients who had been taking diazepam for some years had damaged brains.

In 1982, the *Journal of Psychology* reported that if a patient takes diazepam, he won't be able to remember things he learns while taking the drug unless he takes it again. This discovery had massive implications for those patients taking the drug – and attempting to stop it.

In 1982, a report in *Digestive Diseases and Sciences* showed that diazepam may cause liver damage.

In 1983, a report in *Drug Reaction Bulletin* showed that between 11% and 20% of drivers involved in traffic accidents were taking tranquillisers.

A report in *Medical Biology* in 1982 showed that the calming effect of diazepam is counteracted by caffeine.

Between 1964 and 1982, the Committee on Safety of Medicines in London received reports of well over 100 different side effects said to be related to the use of diazepam.

In my book *Life Without Tranquillisers* (1985) I wrote: 'if you are looking for a crutch and you intend to choose between tobacco and benzodiazepines then you'll probably be better off choosing tobacco.'

In the 1980s, when I was the medical columnist for *The Star* newspaper in the UK, I ran a long campaign about benzodiazepines.

In 1988, speaking in the UK's House of Commons, the Parliamentary Secretary for Health, introduced stricter controls for benzodiazepines and changed the classification of the drugs in an attempt to force doctors to treat them with more respect. She said: 'Dr Vernon Coleman's articles, to which I refer with approval, raised concern about these important matters'. It had taken 15 years of campaigning to force through these changes.

Appendix Four

Normal Pressure Hydrocephalus

In the memory entitled *The Case of the Wobbly Film Star*, I describe how my patient Mrs Ruthvens was diagnosed as suffering from a disorder called Normal Pressure Hydrocephalus. This disorder was first described in 1965 by Hakim and Adams but even now, over half a century later, it is still wildly under-diagnosed. As of 2017, it was estimated that thousands of patients who have been diagnosed as suffering from Alzheimer's disease or another untreatable form of dementia were, in fact, suffering from normal pressure hydrocephalus and could be cured with a simple operation. The disorder is officially described as 'rare' but it has been reliably estimated that up to 4% of all those over the age of 65 are suffering from it. Normal pressure hydrocephalus is undoubtedly the commonest, treatable cause of major disability and mental incapacity among the elderly. Readers who would like to know more might like to take a look at my website www.vernoncoleman.com where there are articles dealing with the disorder and explaining why it is still so rarely diagnosed or treated. My monograph *Millions of Alzheimer's Patients Have Been Misdiagnosed (And Could Be Cured)* is available as an ebook on Amazon.

Appendix Five

The Story of Medicine

In the memory entitled *The Case of the Wobbly Film Star* I mentioned that it was my ambition to write a book about the history of medicine. I eventually managed to do this. My book *The Story of Medicine* is available as an ebook on Amazon.

And finally…
I hope you have enjoyed this book. If you did so then I would be very grateful if you would spare a moment to write a short review.
Thank you
Vernon Coleman

Made in the USA
Middletown, DE
20 May 2021